DOG LEADERSHIP ACADEMY

Beyond Treats: Revolutionary Dog Training for Lasting Behaviour Change

A Story-Based Force Free Compassionate Dog Training Guide

DOG LEADERSHIP
GUIDE SERIES

First published by Dog Leadership Academy 2025

Copyright © 2025 by Dog Leadership Academy

This novel is entirely a work of fiction. The names, characters and incidents portrayed in it are the work of the author's imagination. Any resemblance to actual persons, living or dead, events or localities is entirely coincidental.

Dog Leadership Academy asserts the moral right to be identified as the author of this work.

Dog Rescues are the unsung heroes of the dog world. They save dogs from death every day. There is never enough money to go around and vet bills are not cheap. A portion of the money from this book will be donated to support dog rescues. Everyone wins, especially the dogs that need our help.

You are permitted to resell this book (PDF available to members at www.dogleadershipacademy.com) and keep all the money as long as it is on your private website, and not on a major platform like Amazon, Google, Apple, etc.

Second edition

ISBN (paperback): 978-1-7637735-1-6
ISBN (hardcover): 978-1-7637735-9-2
ISBN (digital): 978-1-7637735-0-9

Editing by Carol Anne

This book was professionally typeset on Reedsy. Find out more at reedsy.com

Beyond Treats

A Story-Based Force-Free Compassionate Dog Training Guide

Dog Leadership Training #1

Revolutionary Dog Training for Lasting Behavior Change

GEORGE TRAN
DOG BEHAVIOURIST

This book would not have been possible without the unwavering faith of thousands of clients who believe in me.

I am who I am because of my Mother, Mai Tran, who is and will always be the wind beneath my wings.

I also want to extend my heartfelt gratitude to my beautiful wife, Carol Anne, who has steadfastly stood by my side through thick and thin.

And to my pit bull, Buddy, who helped me start on this path.

Contents

Foreword — iii
A Complete and Holistic Solution — viii
Please Help Me Save More Dogs — x
Don't Have Time to Read? — xi
Meet Emily — xii

1. I Quit! — 1
2. The Opportunity — 5
3. The Apprenticeship — 12
4. The Jailbreak — 19
5. Rewarding For the Right Behaviour — 29
6. Marker Training and the Dog Park — 36
7. Leadership Based Training — 42
8. The Leadership Walk — 55
9. Comfort vs. Correction — 68
10. Levelling Up, Drills and Staging Events for Training — 77
11. Wax On, Wax Off — 87
12. Jumping on Guests — 94
13. Use of Corrections, Timely Guidance and Property Destruction — 100
14. Recall Training — 106
15. The Road Trip — 111
16. The Panacea — 118
17. True Obedience — 122
18. Impulse Control, Delayed Gratification and Pack Hierarchy — 129
19. Fight or Flight - Dog Reactivity and Fear Based Aggression — 141
20. Don't Stop Believing — 150
21. The First Client — 157

22	The Barker	163
23	The Insecure Jealous Boyfriend	173
24	The Kindness Paradox	184
25	The Behaviourist	197
26	Epilogue	200
27	Who Was Buddy?	202
28	Additional Resources	207
29	Help Me Save More Dogs	211
30	Also By George Tran	213
31	Backed by Science	215

Foreword

With over 40 years as a dog trainer, I've observed a concerning rise in dogs being euthanised, often as a result of the shortcomings of exclusively positive, treat-based training methods. George's book emerges as a much-needed voice of reason in the dog training arena. It's not only insightful but also easily relatable. I strongly recommend this book to anyone looking to enhance their bond with their dogs without an excessive dependence on treats.-
   Gaz Jackson - Author

5 Stars
Beyond Treats takes a heartfelt, story-based dive into dog training, where empathy meets structure, and leadership replaces force. Told through Emily's journey--an aspiring dog trainer navigating her bond with a troubled rescue, Buddy--the book combines an emotional narrative with Tran's leadership-based dog training philosophy. It's a must-read for those frustrated by conventional treat-reliant methods, offering a refreshing alternative that centers around mutual respect and lasting behavioral change.
  - Titan Literary Review

It was a heartwarming story of a woman finding her way and finding happiness. A story of hope and believing you can make a difference. It's a book that will lift you up and help you see so many positives in life. A hugely recommended read if you're a dog lover, or even if you're considering going into a Behaviourist or Trainer profession. If you want to know more about training your dog, George Tran is your guy!
- Emily Quinn - A Quintillion Words Review

The lessons in the book are relevant for dog parents looking for practical, compassionate, and humane methods for training a well-behaved and happy pet. Tran's insights will also help professional trainers improve their training techniques and achieve better results for their clients, both human and canine.
- Maileen Hamto - Reedsy Discovery Review

I have just finished reading your book and it is amazing!!!!! I honestly could not put the book down at all. I loved the summaries at the end of every chapter. It's definitely a book I will cherish with me forever and will continue to recommend to friends and family. It's extremely insightful and I am privileged to be able to have the opportunity to read such a profound book. Thank you for writing a masterpiece! ♥-
    Eve S

I highly recommend anyone who has or is thinking of getting a dog to read this very informative story about dog behaviour. George explains in plain English how to solve all kinds of annoying dog behaviours in simple ways. He explains why a dog may do certain things and how to change it. He understands dogs and how to help

both owner and dogs create a mutually beneficial relationship. This is a must read for all dog lovers young and old to improve our relationships with our wonderful companions.-
    Virginia H

"Beyond Treats" is very well written. It not only has a story line to keep the reader interested but is an excellent training tool. It emphasises the importance of leadership, patience and consistency which are so vital in training any dog.

George Tran's wealth of knowledge is evident throughout the book. It is such an easy read. I would recommend it to anyone wanting a well behaved pup.-
    Kerry W

Why Read This Book?

If you are struggling with your dog's behaviour or simply want to strengthen the bond you share, *Beyond Treats* is the guide you need. With over a decade of hands-on experience, I have developed a unique leadership-based approach to help owners gain respect from their dogs and inspire them to obey without relying on treats, fear, or force.

There are those who believe in the old-school dominance-based style of training, where violence, fear, and threats are used to exact compliance. And there are those who believe that saying no to a dog is tantamount to abuse. No wonder dog owners are confused. My desire is to inspire you to be better and show you a better way to lead your dog.

Are you frustrated with your dog's behaviour? Confused by the conflicting information offered online? Tired of your dog not being obedient and fed up with constantly bribing them with treats for every command? Then this book will show you how to be a leader your dog respects and want to please.

I became a behaviourist because I was frustrated by seeing so many dogs euthanised due to bad advice, even from so-called professional dog trainers. Dog owners often receive conflicting advice, making it difficult to know what truly works. My mission is to help families and save dogs by providing clear, compassionate guidance. My desire is to inspire you to be better and show you a more effective way to lead your dog.

If you're tired of trying every trick without success, you're not alone. Many owners feel overwhelmed and discouraged. Beyond Treats offers a practical, proven method developed from over a decade of experience successfully helping more than 1,000 dogs. You'll tap into your dog's natural desire to please, much like a child seeking a parent's approval.

You'll follow Emily, a fictional dog owner at her wits' end with a dog that society had given up on. Through her story, you'll see dog behaviour differently and learn how understanding the science behind every growl, bark, and wag.

As someone who is often recommended by vets across Australia for clients considering euthanasia, I know how vital it is to provide the right support before it's too late. I have spoken at many dog events, sharing my insights and advocating for a compassionate, informed approach to dog training. Through my book, public speaking, and advocacy, my desire is to change the narrative around dog behaviour, showing that issues can be resolved without medication or surrender.

So I invite you to join me and get started on the journey to a more obedient and well-behaved dog through leadership and respect.

George Tran
Dog Behaviourist

P.S. Dog rescues are at the forefront of saving dogs; they are the true unsung heroes of the dog world. They are always the first to help when someone needs to surrender a dog, yet the last to receive financial support for vet bills. Unfortunately, there is often not enough funding to support them. This is why **a significant portion of the proceeds from this book and venture goes to helping dog rescues around the world.**

A Complete and Holistic Solution

"Beyond Treats" introduces a leadership-based philosophy that transforms how you connect with your dog. This book uses a story-driven approach to move beyond treat-based training, fostering respect, trust, and enduring behavioral changes.

I've crafted "Beyond Treats" in a narrative style to make the concepts of leadership-based dog training both relatable and engaging. By diving into Emily's journey with her rescue dog, Buddy, you'll explore real-life scenarios and solutions, gaining a profound understanding of these principles.

I recognize that not everyone has the time or inclination for a story. If you're looking for something more straightforward, here's what we offer:

- **The Dog Leadership Training Guide:** A comprehensive, no-nonsense manual filled with actionable strategies to tackle everyday behavior challenges. **Free to access.**
- **The Beyond Treats Companion Workbook**: Provides step-by-step exercises designed to enhance trust and respect. **Also free.**

Additionally, we've introduced **My Behaviourist**, an AI-powered canine expert, offering personalized advice whenever you need it, **at no cost**.

Together, these resources give you the tools, knowledge, and insight needed to address issues like leash pulling, anxiety, aggression, and more. They're designed to empower you to become the leader your dog truly deserves.

Visit **www.dogleadershipacademy.com** to access these free resources and begin your journey towards a stronger, more harmonious relationship with your dog. Let's build a future where dogs and their families flourish together.

You can also find "Beyond Treats" and its companions at your favorite online bookstores, available in print or Kindle format.

```
"George, you have transformed Chloe. She was so much calmer after
we started practicing your exercises--it was like night and day!
Now, she's cool as a cucumber, even in situations that used to
stress her out.  Your techniques are incredibly easy to follow and
unbelievably effective. We can't thank you enough!"
  - Michelle and Roger - and Chloe
```

Please Help Me Save More Dogs

The purpose of this book is to help educate the world on a better way to train dogs that is both effective, **force free and humane so that they do not get surrendered or euthanised due to behaviours**.

If you find value in the insights and information contained within these pages, please forward this book or **tell at least two other people who might benefit from it**. You are invited to **write a review of this book** so more people know about the valuable knowledge shared in this book.

Non-profit organizations and dog rescue groups are especially encouraged to distribute copies of this book to adopters, foster families, and other stakeholders.

For those interested in obtaining printed versions at wholesale prices, please reach out to info@dogleadershipacademy.com.

Don't Have Time to Read ?

Buy the Audiobook.

Get the MP3 so you can send it to your friends and family.
Come to: www.dogleadershipacademy.com.

Or you can buy it on Audible, Google and Apple, and any other major online audiobook platform.

Come to: https://books2read.com/u/baXwoy

Meet Emily

Quitting my job to save dogs was the best thing I ever did. My name is Emily. For years, my life was on what felt like a never-ending treadmill. Every day was a repetition of the last – the same complaints, the same thankless work. I was a store manager at a major grocery retailer, a job that I had come to loathe. It paid the bills, and for a long time, that had been enough.

Then, one day, I met him. He was strong, handsome, and intelligent. His unwavering loyalty was endearing, and I found solace in his quiet company during those cold winter months. He was everything a girl could ever dream of.

His name was Buddy, my mix-breed mutt. He wasn't just a dog, he was my dog– a living, breathing symbol of my decision to finally break free from my monotonous life and pursue my dream of working with dogs.

This is our story, a story about more than just dog training, it's about the power of change and the journey toward self-discovery; it's a story about stepping out of the comfort zone and embracing the unpredictable; about finding love where you least expect it, and about the incredible bond between a human and her dog.

So, if you've ever felt stuck, ever felt the urge to break out of your shell and follow your passion, or if you simply love dogs as much as I do, then this story is for you. Join me and Buddy as we navigate the ups and downs of dog behaviour and discover, along the way, that sometimes, the biggest transformations come on four legs.

1

I Quit!

They say that you die spiritually at twenty-five and your body just takes the rest of your days to finish the job. It happened to me. I had given up hope, just living on autopilot. I was a zombie, merely going through the motions.

At six in the morning, my alarm jolted me awake with the strains of Journey's 'Don't Stop Believin''. My day had begun. Again. I dragged myself out of bed, dressed, and prepared to face another day of monotony, to deal with thankless, rude, and angry customers.

As a child, having a dog was out of the question. My mother forbade it. 'When you can look after yourself, only then can you consider bringing a child or a dog into this house,' she'd firmly stated.

My mother, hardened by life, and I, the dreamer, rarely saw eye to eye. Once I graduated, I moved from one job to another, each one more uninspiring than the last. When I met Ryan, I was young and naive - young and stupid more like. Ryan was everything I thought I wanted: cocky, confident, flashy, and I thought he wanted me. More precisely, he wanted a maid.

His controlling nature slowly morphed into abuse and, when I tried to break free, it only got worse. Yes, hindsight is twenty/twenty, and I learned that lesson the hard way.

As I drove to work, the lyrics of 'Don't Stop Believin'' echoed through my mind, refusing to be silenced. At a red light, I found myself humming along, lost in the melody when it occurred to me, when did I stop believing?

BEYOND TREATS: REVOLUTIONARY DOG TRAINING FOR LASTING BEHAVIOUR CHANGE

When did I stop believing in my dreams, in my potential? When did I let the dreams of that innocent, hopeful girl be replaced by the harsh realities of my dull, uninspiring life? This wasn't how I envisioned my life at twenty-nine.

In that moment, sitting in my car, the traffic lights blinking in the early morning haze, I felt a deep, resounding frustration. My life was a series of compromises, decisions made out of necessity rather than desire.

'I hate my life,' I thought. The words hit me with a surprising intensity. The routine, the monotony, the endless cycle of dissatisfaction – I was done with it all. Adulting, as it happened, really sucks. This veil of discontent enveloped me as I parked and headed into the store.

Later, as I was instructing one of my staff about restocking, I heard a shrill, "I want to talk to your manager!" I inhaled deeply, pasted a pleasant expression onto my face, and approached the dissatisfied customer. I politely inquired, "I'm the manager here. How may I help you?"

The customer, a short, prim and proper woman with a seriously starched 1960s hairdo, seething with anger, thrust an empty soup container in my direction, and demanded a refund. She had bought it from our store and claimed to have found a hair at the bottom of her bowl as she was finished her meal.

I calmly and professionally explained our company refund policy to her. Unfortunately, we couldn't issue a refund since she had already consumed the soup. Her reaction to this was less than pleasant.

With a look of disgust, a scream of frustration, she, to my shock, flung the empty container at my face and stormed off.

It was then that something inside me snapped. "I'm so done." That was the day I handed in my two-week notice.

As the days of that fortnight crawled by, 'Don't Stop Believin'' played on an endless loop in my head. Perhaps it was a sign of good things to come.

In anticipation of my last day, I spent my evenings curled on the lounge binge-watching videos and dreaming of my next career move. Somehow, I found myself deep-diving into dog training videos. I was fascinated by the technique of positive only training. It was touted as the latest, science-backed approach to dog training. It had to be good, right? So, I dove in and absorbed as much as I could, enveloping myself in a world that had always fascinated me. The stress of the upcoming last day was starting to ebb, replaced by a cautious hope. I had forgotten what that felt like.

In my quest for knowledge, I stumbled upon a dog behaviourist based in Sydney, Australia named George Tran. He had worked with thousands of clients struggling with dog behaviour issues, and his approach intrigued me. Rather than all-positive, his approach was leadership based training.

I followed George, learned about his work, his methods, and his philosophy. I followed his social media platforms, watched so many of his videos, and read about his success in training and rehabilitating dogs, even those with extreme behaviour issues. It was inspiring. His teachings began to reshape my understanding of dogs and natural dog behaviour. I began to feel something I'd been missing for a while – excitement, and a sense of purpose.

As I immersed myself in the world of dogs, I began following several dog rescue groups. To my dismay, I found the reality heartbreaking. Every rescue was overwhelmed, struggling to accommodate more dogs. The recent pandemic had led to a surge in dog adoptions as people sought companionship during isolation. But as society returned to normal, the pendulum swung the other way, with dogs being surrendered at an alarming rate.

This tragic situation has been exacerbated by the ongoing housing crisis. With inflation soaring and interest rates climbing, many people have been forced to downsize or move in with family, often at the expense of their dogs. As a result, thousands of dogs are being surrendered or euthanised.

What struck me as even more disturbing was the underlying cause of many of these surrenders: behavioural issues. Unsocialised 'pandemic puppies' struggled with problems like barking and leash reactivity, making them difficult to rehome. Sadly, most people are unaware that dog behaviourists even exist. When they encounter behaviour issues, their first instinct is to consult a vet, who often diagnoses these problems as anxiety and prescribes anti-anxiety drugs. This is like going to an electrician for a plumbing problem. The result is a population of unruly, untrained, and over medicated dogs, whose issues could have been addressed with the right behavioural guidance.

The enormity of the problem is overwhelming, but it has only strengthened my resolve. I am determined to learn everything I can about dog behaviour and training so that, in my own small way, I can make a difference.

Prefer a Traditional Format?

If the story format isn't for you, we've got you covered.

Download the **free** *Dog Leadership Training Guide*—a traditional, in-depth resource that dives straight into the principles of dog leadership training.

Visit www.dogleadershipacademy.com to get your free copy today!

You can also download it from your favourite online ebook retailer like Amazon, Google, Apple and Barnes and Noble. Look for *"Dog Leadership Training Guide"*.

# 2

The Opportunity

Maybe it was the eyes, those sad, pleading eyes. Or perhaps it was his overall demeanour, the unmistakable air of a creature who had been let down time and again yet, when I saw Buddy, a dog at the pound, on Facebook, something inside me shattered.

Buddy looked lost, sad, and utterly broken. Worse, he was on the kill list, slated for euthanasia. They were asking for pledges, for help to save his life.

I felt a connection to Buddy that I couldn't quite put into words. It was as if we were two broken souls, let down by the world, by humans. Buddy, like me, had stopped believing.

Driven by an impulse I hadn't felt in years, I decided to meet Buddy. What's the harm in just looking, after all?

I had no idea then that this decision would change my life.

The drive to the pound was a whirlwind of nervous anticipation. What was I doing? I had never owned a dog before, let alone one with potential behavioural issues. Who did stuff like this? Me, apparently.

All I had was hope, the naive dreams of making a difference, and a stubborn determination that wouldn't let me back down.

From an outsider's perspective, Buddy was just another dog, yet for Buddy, it was a matter of life and death. If I didn't step up, if I didn't care, he would die. That was a reality I couldn't bear to face.

I arrived at the pound and was instantly overwhelmed by the sheer number of dogs needing homes. Each one was barking, acting out in a desperate plea for attention, screaming, "Please, pick me. Take me home. Save my life."

I fought the tears that threatened to spill. The scene triggered a deep-seated memory, one I had long buried, back to my childhood at the orphanage, with the same hope in my own heart - to be chosen, to be taken home, and to belong. I remembered the devastation when I wasn't picked, when kids were returned, when adoptions didn't work out.

That forgotten memory hit me like a wave. I stumbled and held firmly to the concrete wall as I breathed deeply through this unexpected moment of kinship with these desperate creatures.

When I reached the desk and inquired about Buddy, I received quizzical looks. "Really? You're interested in THAT one? Are you sure? He failed his assessment for rehoming because he's aggressive with other dogs."

"Yes," I replied firmly. "I'm here to see Buddy."

They led me to his cell, a foreboding sign hung on his cell, 'Warning. He Bites. Scheduled for Euthanasia.'

I asked the ranger for more information about Buddy. He shrugged, "Same story as half these dogs here, Buddy was a pandemic dog that had been left in the backyard. He was eventually surrendered because his owner didn't have time for him anymore. Why are you interested in this particular dog? You know he has some issues, right?"

"I saw his photo online and I'm curious. May I spend some time with Buddy?"

He responded with a dismissive, "Knock yourself out. Take your time. He isn't going anywhere. Just be careful, he has a bad reputation."

The ranger's tone, his indifference, filled me with sadness and anger. As I observed Buddy, he didn't strike me as dangerous. Defeated, yes, not a threat, though. I settled down beside his enclosure, simply sharing his space. At first, I sat quietly while Buddy stood at the furthest corner of his cell from me. I found myself softly humming and tapping my toes, lost in my head. When I realised the song was 'Don't Stop Believin', I began to whisper the lyrics aloud. Peripherally, I noticed Buddy cock his head to the side, watching me. After several verses, Buddy slowly approached and cautiously sniffed me. I took a chance to look him straight in the eyes – those deep, warm, brown eyes.

I rummaged in my pocket and pulled a handful of chicken jerky treats. He was wary at first, his eyes darting between my hand and my eyes, measuring me. Eventually, he sniffed my hand and allowed me to feed him. From that moment, we began a subtle dance of trust. The first wag of his tail felt like a victory, a spark of hope with the impact of a full New Year fireworks display in my heart. I brought out my phone and snapped a few pictures of him.

That was the moment I knew – I couldn't let this dog die. I simply couldn't. I had to save Buddy. I reached between the bars, rubbed the bridge of his muzzle, and whispered, "I'm going to do my best, Buddy. Somehow, I intend to find a way."

When I approached the ranger about adopting Buddy, I was informed that he wasn't available for adoption because he failed his assessment. He was declared a dangerous dog which required sponsorship from a behaviourist or a rescue group.

Undeterred, I gave the ranger my phone number, insisting that I would save Buddy's life. I implored him to give me a few days to arrange things. The ranger and the desk volunteer shared sceptical looks, as if I had lost my mind, or they'd heard that a thousand times. They simply responded with a noncommittal, "OK. Whatever."

Once back in my car, I let the tears flow. "What have I gotten myself into? I am so out of my league."

Why Buddy? Of all the dogs at the shelter, why had I connected with him? A dog with behavioural issues and a reputation. Or, was he simply misunderstood? Was it all bravado to cloak fear and disappointment? I shook my head, dragged my sleeve across my face to absorb the tears, and started the engine. It didn't matter. I promised Buddy. I was going to do all I could for him. The question now was, who could I turn to for help?

As I drove home, I began to review all the videos I'd watched and it hit me, George Tran, the behaviourist I had been following. He was in Sydney, just like I was. Maybe he could help save Buddy. I spent the rest of the drive rehearsing my appeal to him. I parked in front of my house, brought up his social media profile, and dialled his number right in the car.

To my surprise, he picked up. I was so shocked, everything I planned to say evaporated and I tearfully told him about Buddy, about my commitment to saving his life, and my dream of becoming a dog trainer to help save more dogs from ending up in the pound. Instead of mocking me, he listened. I finished my plea with, "I know it's probably crazy for someone who never had a dog to want Buddy with all his problems. I know. I also know that everyone has problems, and I feel so sure that Buddy and I could be each other's solutions to some of those problems, if we had the help of someone like you. Please, Mr. Tran, is there any way you could help us?"

Something in my story, or perhaps my determination to save Buddy, resonated with George. He explained that he occasionally took on apprentices, but it was a paid program. It was a significant sum, more than I could afford. He also told me that he simply didn't have any space at his facility, so taking Buddy in was out of the question.

"Emily," George began, "I've had many people approach me with stories, with dreams, and with aspirations. They all want to be dog trainers, they all have a 'challenging dog' they want to save. Let me tell you, though, this path is not easy. It's not just about loving dogs; it's about understanding them, it's about commitment, patience, and sometimes making tough decisions."

I swallowed hard, trying to keep my emotions in check. "I understand, Mr. Tran. I'm willing to do whatever it takes. I believe in Buddy, and I believe in myself."

George sighed, "In the past, I've trained individuals for free, thinking they were serious about the program. Time and again, they've let me down. It ended up being a waste of time and resources because they didn't take it seriously, partly because they had no skin in the game."

During the following hour, George meticulously dissected every aspect of my motivations, my history with dogs, my character, and my future goals. Every answer I provided, he countered with another question, pushing me to dig deeper and truly understand my own passions.

As we spoke, I could sense George becoming increasingly impressed with my unwavering commitment to Buddy. "Normally," he admitted, "I would have said no to taking on another apprentice at this time, yet your passion for this dog, your dedication to his well-being, it's evident and rare."

He then introduced me to the concept of All In. George explained, "The reason most people never achieve their dreams is that they only give half of themselves. They try, yet never fully commit." He emphasised the power of unwavering dedication, saying, "Providence favours the bold." He said, "Remember what Yoda said, 'Try not. Do…or do not. There is no try.'"

George shared that the secret to his success had always been his laser-focused determination. "Once I set my mind on something," he told me, "I don't waver. I don't give up. I go all in." His words resonated deeply and realised the level of commitment and dedication I needed to bring to this journey.

As our conversation drew to a close, I felt both drained and invigorated. "Emily, your passion is evident. I'm willing to admit you to my apprenticeship program,however, the fee is non-negotiable. It's an investment in your future and a testament to your dedication. If you can figure out how to make that commitment, I'll sponsor Buddy and train you."

I thanked George and promised to get back to him as soon as possible. Becoming a Behaviourist would be just like any other professional endeavour, be it hairstyling, lab work, or culinary arts, there's a cost to education. Whether through Community College, TAFE, or other vocational programs, there's always a fee. Why should dog training be any different? Especially if I aimed to tackle challenges like human aggression or dog reactivity, I'd need comprehensive training. This wasn't just a hobby; it was a career change.

"Emily," I said to myself. "You're going to become a dog behaviourist!" The notion snapped neatly into a hole I never knew I had and filled it perfectly. I sat in my car for a whole minute, grinning like I'd won the lottery until it also dawned on me that I had to figure out how to come up with the money for the training… and fast! Buddy's life was on a clock. I slumped forward and rested my head on the steering wheel. Obstacles. I needed to talk to someone.

"Mum," I said aloud. "I need to talk to mum." I sat up straight, started the engine, and drove to my adoptive mum's house. The woman that had been my rock, my staunch advocate from the moment we locked eyes in that orphanage, she always had ideas. Even though she was retired from her career in automotive repair, her mechanical, logical mind was as sharp as ever. The house, much like her, bore the marks of hard work and dedication. It was modest, well-kept, with a small garden out front that she tended to with the same meticulous care she once gave to cars.

As I parked, her head popped up from behind a hedge of gardenias. Her smile was warm and wide, yet her sharp eyes narrowed a bit. "Emily," she said, pulling me into a tight embrace. "It's been too long. Come in, you can tell me what's on your mind over tea."

As we settled into the living room, I began to share the recent events of my life, including my journey with Buddy. She listened intently and, when I finished, she took a deep breath, "Emily, how can you do this? You can barely take care of yourself. You've just quit your job, and now you want to adopt a dog that will need a lot of attention to settle into your life."

I felt a pang of frustration, "mum, I'm twenty-nine. I'm not a child anymore."

She quirked an eyebrow, "Honey, I don't care if you're sixty, you'll always be my child."

I sighed, too exhausted to argue the point. As I looked around the room, I was reminded of the sacrifices she had made for me. The walls were adorned with photos of our family, and I could see the pride in her eyes in every picture. She had always placed my needs and the needs of the family before hers. She had worked hard all her life as an auto mechanic, a woman in a man's world, back at that time. A woman who had commanded the respect of everyone in her workplace through sheer will, guts, and raw determination.

Mum leaned over, refilled my cup, and cleared her throat. "I have some fun news. I've finally booked a cruise!" She pulled a flyer from a stack of magazines and pushed it toward me. "It's not until next year, so I'm trying to curb my enthusiasm. I'm really excited, though."

She had always dreamt of going on a cruise, a dream she had set aside for years.

Her excitement was contagious, "Good on ya, mum, you deserve it! Tell me all about it!"

As the last drop of tea was drunk, our conversation circled back to me and my plans for Buddy. I explained about George Tran and the sponsorship predicament, including the apprenticeship fee. mum was outraged, calling it exorbitant. I explained that it was comparable to other places, and George's program was hands-on, the start of a new career for me, and, most importantly, my best chance to save Buddy.

She pushed back, challenging me. Was I sure I wanted to spend my days working with potentially dangerous animals? How could I be assured of a regular income? She tried to talk me out of it, suggesting that I settle for a different job instead, maybe a quiet desk job far away from dirty and possibly dangerous animals and customers throwing soup cans. What hurt most was her lack of faith in me that I'd fail with George. I swallowed the tears that threatened to spill. I wasn't going to let her see me cry, like the child I was when she adopted me all those years ago. I steeled myself, narrowed my eyes and quietly affirmed, "I will figure it out. I will find the money, I will apply myself, and I will save Buddy. Watch me!"

She nodded. I helped her tidy up from tea, and I left her house, more resolute than ever.

At home, desperation set in. I realised that even if I couldn't keep Buddy, I could at least attempt to save his life. I began posting about his situation, sharing his photos on social media, with the hope that someone might step up. I also tried reaching out to several rescue organisations.

Each effort seemed to hit a brick wall until I spoke with Jan from Pound Jailbreakers. Jan mentioned a well-off friend who might be able to help. She'd do what she could and let me know if they came through. I thanked her with gratitude, yet little optimism.

Before bed, I set one of the photos of Buddy as my phone's background. I looked into those hopeful eyes and whispered, "Hang in there, Buddy. I'm working on it."

3

The Apprenticeship

The next morning, my alarm sang 'Don't Stop Believin'' at the rude and unnecessary hour of six in the morning. I reminded myself that I was no longer working and didn't need the early morning wake-up call. Exhausted and feeling defeated, I dragged myself out of bed, brewed some coffee, and tried to gather my thoughts while making breakfast.

My mind kept circling back to Buddy. I knew I could train him if given the chance. While George seemed amenable to sponsor Buddy's release, my big challenge was coming up with the money for the necessary apprenticeship and Buddy's adoption fee. George was an extremely busy person, and it was unreasonable to expect him to train me for free, yet I had wracked my brains late into the night as to a source of funding, to no avail. Getting a credit card or a loan was out of the question, given that I had just quit my job.

After a second cup of coffee – for valour – I checked my email to see if any of the leads I had pursued came through. I quickly clicked on the message from Jan from Pound Jailbreakers. She had spoken to her benefactor friend about my situation, and he was considering helping. She said she'd let me know. That was a thread of hope, albeit a thin one.

Rather than continue to obsess over my inbox, I decided to catch up with Sally, an old friend who'd recently adopted a puppy. We hadn't hung out as much as we used to, everyone's lives seem to be on fast forward these days.

I arrived at the café a tad early, so I checked my social media feed while awaiting Sally. To my surprise, my post about Buddy had garnered quite a bit of attention. The flurry of supportive comments and number of shared posts gave me a glimmer of hope.

It was a blissful relief from my worries to chat and laugh with Sally over lunch. We had been friends since school and, though we rarely had time to physically see each other, ours was a relationship that immediately picked up from where we left off, like no time had passed. The biggest addition to Sally's life was her recently adopted baby cavoodle, Benji. He was a wild, excitable, fluffy bundle of chocolate covered espresso beans with golden eyes. She was completely smitten with her naughty little pup.

"I've spent the money on a series of obedience classes for Benji. I just wish they were helping more. We go every week, and he's just as naughty as ever. I hope he grows out of it. He still tears the cushions, digs the garden, and he's a bit of an embarrassment on the leash. That's why I left him at home today. He barks at everything, and he just exhausts me. They told me to give him treats when he's a good boy, and if he doesn't listen, to wave the treat in front of his face to distract him.," she relayed sadly.

"I'm so sorry, Sally. It sounds like the classes aren't working, and that's frustrating. How are they telling you to handle Benji?"

Sally took a deep breath before diving into the details. "The trainer is all about the treats-only approach. They said it's the latest scientific method, developed by researchers from top universities. The idea is that you never say 'no' to a dog. According to them, there's absolutely no need to correct a dog, even if they misbehave. Instead, you just use treats and positive reinforcements to reward the behaviour you want, like when they stop misbehaving and turning your back or ignoring the inappropriate behaviour. It's kind of like permissive parenting approach, but for dogs. The problem is, if the dog is bouncing off the walls and always into mischief, there's rarely a 'correct behaviour' moment for me to reward.

"When I confronted the trainer with my concerns," Sally continued, "He assured me Benji would come around, and I needed patience. I told him that we had dogs when I was a kid and that my parents disciplined them just like they disciplined me and he recoiled. Truly, the man gasped aloud and clutched his chest!" Sally mimicked the gesture and we both giggled.

"Wow!?!?" I grinned.

"I know, right? It was a good thing I was too gobsmacked to laugh right then. With his hand still over his heart, he launched into dire warnings about people who discipline their dogs. He was quite adamant that training methods involving discipline and corrections will lead to fearful, shut down dogs.

"When I told him that my parents' older dogs often were the ones that kept the newest additions in line, he shook his head vehemently and explained that the latest science has debunked the effectiveness of 'pack training.' He said it was an outdated model. He insisted that positive reinforcement and treats were the only way to go. It may take a few years for Benji to truly listen and respond, and I may have to offer ever increasingly delightful treats, yet he insisted it would eventually work."

I quirked an eyebrow. "So, the thousands of years of dogs raising and training their own is wrong? How can that be scientifically proven? And more delightful treats? Are you meant to roast pheasant and potatoes for the dog?"

Sally sighed, "I'm losing faith, and I don't know what to do."

"I feel ya," I consoled. "I've had my own frustrations centred around a dog."

I told Sally about Buddy's situation and my dream of becoming George's apprentice. I explained my intentions to save Buddy and all the challenges that came with it.

Sally was enthusiastic about my plan, offering much-needed emotional support that was far more encouraging than my mother's reaction. After lunch, Sally suggested we pick up Benji from her house and allow him to expend some energy at the local dog park. I waited in the car while Sally ran into the house and was dragged out by Benji. We fastened his harness into the backseat and drove to the park.

Benji, cute as a button, was off the charts excited. About everything. Chocolate covered espresso beans packed less energy than this little cavoodle. When Sally released him from his leash, Benji bound into the park. He was a whirlwind of excitement running and jumping on other dogs. I noticed he seemed to be bothering a German Shepherd who appeared uninterested in play. Benji dodged in and out of the shepherd's space, barking and wagging his tail like mad. Eventually, the shepherd had enough of Benji's antics. He pinned Benji to the ground, growling loudly and showing his teeth.

We both dashed over, anticipating a potential fight. By the time we reached them, the dogs had already gone their separate ways. Sally looked quite upset, believing her dog had been attacked.

Benji was physically fine and even seemed a bit more reserved. He sat calmly by Sally's side while she fussed over him. He was, for a change, being a good boy.

"Sally," I offered, "That wasn't an attack. That was a warning. Don't you see? Benji was being a nuisance. He wouldn't leave the German Shepherd alone, so the shepherd responded forcefully. Did you notice that they both simply walked away afterwards? And Benji has been calm and well adjusted since. I think that the German Shepherd was teaching Benji how to behave more appropriately."

Sally was startled by my observation and paused. "I hadn't considered it from that angle."

"Could it be that dogs are actually better at training each other naturally than scientists with degrees?" I wondered aloud.

~~~

The incident at the dog park with the German Shepherd and Benji continued to replay in my mind. Dogs have their own language, their own way of communicating. They don't have words, and they certainly don't have treats to reward each other for good behaviour. So, how do they set boundaries? How do they correct each other?

I closed my eyes and imagined myself as a dog, trying to communicate with another dog that was bothering me. At first, I'd probably try to move away, hoping the other dog would take the hint. But what if it didn't? What if it kept coming at me, ignoring my signals of discomfort?

I'd probably growl, a low rumble from deep within, a clearer warning. If that didn't work, I'd show my teeth, curling my lips to display my displeasure. It's not about aggression, it's about setting boundaries. And if all else failed? I'd probably snap or pin the other dog, much like I'd shove away someone who was invading my personal space. It's a last resort, the ultimate, unmistakable message that enforces, "Enough is enough. Back off!"

I opened my eyes and realised that this was precisely what the German Shepherd had done with Benji. It wasn't an act of aggression, it was a more emphatic form of communication. The Shepherd had tried to avoid Benji, and had given him signals to back off, but Benji, in his puppy enthusiasm, had missed those cues. The pinning was the Shepherd's last resort, his way of saying, "Respect my space."

I began to wonder about all the times we must misinterpret dogs' actions, labelling them as aggressive or problematic when they were merely trying to communicate in the only way they know how. If we took the time to understand their language, to see the world from their perspective, perhaps we'd have fewer misunderstandings and a deeper bond with our canine companions. If I invited someone from a foreign culture to live with me, I'd certainly make the effort to understand their ways of communicating. Dogs deserve the same effort.

This revelation added fuel to my efforts to rescue Buddy. Every passing hour amplified the urgency of his situation, every tick of the clock was a reminder of the limited time Buddy had left. Every time I closed my eyes, I saw his face, those soulful eyes that appealed for a chance at life.

George's words echoed in my mind. His facility was full, and he couldn't take Buddy. The thought of joining George's program was a goal, yet my financial constraints made it an impossibility in the moment. I felt trapped, caught in a situation where every door seemed to be closed to me, and poor Buddy was on the other side of those doors.

I paced around my living room, wracking my brain for a solution. I couldn't bear the thought of Buddy spending another night in the pound, especially knowing that his days were numbered. The reality of the situation was harsh. Pounds and rescues were overflowing, and finding someone willing to take in a dog, especially one with Buddy's reputation, was a daunting task.

I took a deep breath, trying to calm my racing heart. Panicking and wearing a path in my carpet wouldn't help Buddy. I needed to be proactive, to find a solution, no matter how impossible it seemed.

THE APPRENTICESHIP

I grabbed my laptop and began researching. There had to be other rescue organisations, maybe even private individuals, looking to adopt or foster a dog. I spent hours sending out emails, making calls, and reaching out to anyone who might be able to help.

As the evening wore on, my efforts seemed fruitless. Most organisations were full, and those that had space were hesitant to take in a dog like Buddy. I decided to leverage social media, creating another heartfelt post about Buddy's situation, complete with pictures and a detailed account of his story. I pleaded for help, asked for shares, contacts, or any leads that might help me save Buddy.

The outpouring of support from the online community was nothing short of amazing. My phone buzzed with notifications, each chime was a sparkle of hope. The post had gone viral, and the sheer number of shares was a testament to the compassion of strangers. Messages flooded my inbox, each one a mix of encouragement, offers of assistance, and potential leads.

Among the sea of messages, there were those who generously offered to contribute financially to Buddy's cause. Their kindness was overwhelming, and I was deeply moved by their willingness to help a dog they had never met. Others sent information about potential foster homes or rescues that might be willing to take Buddy in, even if it was just temporary.

Amidst the hope, a looming reality shadowed; finding a foster home for Buddy was just one piece of the puzzle. Without a sponsor, be it a rescue organisation or a behaviourist, Buddy's fate remained uncertain. The Pound was unable to release Buddy to just anyone because of his failed assessment. Time was not on my side.

The next morning, with a knot in my stomach, I dialled the Pound's number. The voice on the other end confirmed my worst fears: Buddy was scheduled for euthanasia the following day. The finality of it hit me like a ton of bricks, and I struggled to hold back tears.

In a last-ditch effort, I called my mother, hoping against hope that she might be willing to lend me the money to sponsor Buddy myself. Her response was a cold splash of reality. "Honey, you can't save them all," she pleaded, her voice though sympathetic, felt like a slap. "Why don't you get another, less challenging dog?"

Her words stung. How could she not understand? This wasn't just about a dog, this was about saving a life, a life that deserved a second chance. "I'm not trying to save them all, mum, I'm trying to save one very special soul. With a little luck, maybe Buddy and I can save each other. I've got to go. I have until tonight to find the money and figure out a sponsor." I ended the call with mum and scrolled through social media and email responses, hunting for our miracle.

I felt cornered by circumstances beyond my control. I lacked the right resources, and the clock was ticking. Without a sponsor, Buddy was going to die tomorrow.

At 4pm, my phone suddenly buzzed. I pounced on it and was surprised to hear George Tran, the dog behaviourist, on the line. He explained that a benefactor had come forward, willing to cover the tuition fee for my apprenticeship. There were conditions, however. George would sponsor Buddy for me to adopt, and I'd have to waive any rights to sue the pound because of that failed assessment. George added that he couldn't tell me who the benefactor was and that I'd still have to pay a small part of the fee as a way of having some skin in the game. If I was in, he'd call the Pound before they closed and tell them to cancel the euthanasia order for tomorrow morning. It was an eleventh hour save – talk about cutting it close!

I had given up on miracles, yet now, it seemed all my wishes were coming true. I agreed to the terms without hesitation, dashed over to George's facility to sign all the necessary paperwork, and paid my portion of the apprenticeship fee. He told me he'd meet me at the Pound bright and early the next morning to pick up Buddy. I floated home on a cloud. We saved Buddy!

4

The Jailbreak

At 6 am, the familiar strains of Don't Stop Believin' blared from my alarm, jolting me awake. The song had always held a special place in my heart, a reminder to never give up, no matter how bleak things seemed. Today, its lyrics felt more poignant than ever. I bounced out of bed, singing along with Journey, while I readied myself for the first day of my new life with Buddy.

At this time yesterday, I had been on the brink of despair, speeding toward the end of the road in my quest to save Buddy. Life is full of surprises when we least expect it. Against all odds, things had taken a miraculous turn. The past few days had felt like a dark corridor of closed doors. Today, the sun was shining, the birds were singing, and I was on my way to Buddy.

I arrived at the pound, still singing along with Don't Stop Believin' on repeat. George arrived a few minutes after me. He grabbed a leash from his car, greeted me warmly, and asked, "Are you ready?"

His quiet confidence and warm smile put me at ease. "I am beyond ready! I'm so grateful to you, thank you for this!"

"You'll be doing all the work, I'm here to guide you. If you're ready, let's go fetch Buddy."

We made our way to the Pound's office where we signed a bunch of paperwork to release Buddy. We then proceeded to Buddy's cell. George paused outside, taking a few moments to observe Buddy. His gaze was intense, focused, as if he was trying to read Buddy's soul, to understand the fears and traumas that lay beneath the surface.

With a nod to himself, George entered the cell. He moved with a quiet confidence, pulling a slip lead from his pocket. Buddy, sensing George's calm energy, didn't resist or show any signs of aggression. Within moments, the lead was securely over Buddy's head.

Without any fuss or drama, George led Buddy out of the cell, through the corridors of the pound, and into the daylight. Buddy walked beside him, calm and composed, as if he understood that this was the beginning of a new chapter in his life.

Together, we guided Buddy to George's car where he was secured in a crate in the back for transport to my house. As I watched George interact with Buddy, a sense of gratitude washed over me.

I led the way and, when we arrived at my house, instead of leading Buddy inside, George started a peculiar dance with Buddy on the sidewalk out front. It was nothing like I'd ever seen. He would take a few steps, then turn around and let Buddy catch up. As Buddy approached, George would gently tug the leash, leading him in a different direction.

At first, Buddy was beyond excited, erratic, and full of energy from leaving the pound. But as George continued this dance, Buddy's demeanour shifted. No longer was he overly playful and unruly; he slowed down, becoming more relaxed and submissive. Soon, George had Buddy walking beside him on a loose leash.

I was astounded. I turned to George, asking him to explain the strange dance.

"Welcome to your first lesson, Emily," George announced. "This is known as a Leadership Walk. It's the most crucial and foundational exercise that I teach all my apprentices and clients. For a dog like Buddy, it's vital to establish a working relationship based on respect from the get-go. Many folks treat their dogs as equals, especially when they've just brought them home or if they're rescues. They feel sorry for them, which is one of the biggest mistakes you can make."

"George, I'm struggling to wrap my head around this," I confessed. "I've always believed that every dog, especially those from shelters or rescues, deserve our utmost compassion. What's the harm in treating them delicately? Isn't love the foundation of our bond with them? After all, he's been through so much. Every time I look at him, my heart aches, I feel an immense sense of empathy for him."

"Love and empathy are vital, Emily," George began, his voice gentle yet firm. "They're not the only things dogs need, though. Dogs are like children. They need leadership and guidance, and it's our responsibility to provide that for them."

He leaned in slightly, emphasising his point. "While we can feel sorry for their pasts, it's important to recognise that dogs, especially rescues like Buddy, thrive on structure and boundaries. They need to understand their place in the family like wolves know their place in a pack. When we treat them as our equals, it muddies the waters for them, leading to confusion and anxiety. They need a confident leader, someone they can trust and look up to guide them."

I recalled the story of Sally's obedience trainer. "I heard that pack theory has been debunked?"

A knowing smile played on George's lips. "That's a common misconception," he responded. "David Mech's research on wolf behaviour, which forms the basis of the pack theory, has often been misinterpreted by trainers who heavily rely on just positive reinforcement. Mech himself has tried to rectify this misunderstanding. His theory has been manipulated to fit a certain narrative."

He paused, choosing his words carefully. "Think of it like a family. Suggesting that children don't need guidance or discipline and should be treated as equals doesn't work in a family dynamic. The same goes for a wolf pack."

I absorbed his words, then ventured, "So, being a pet parent is more than just showering them with love and pity. It's about parenting and guidance?"

George nodded affirmatively. "Exactly. Dogs, like Buddy, look to us for direction, much like children look to their parents. It's essential to establish that leadership role from the start. In the canine world, there's always a leader, or even several leaders. If you don't assume that leadership role, Buddy might feel like he needs to step up. That can lead to unwanted behaviours like aggression or disobedience. We want Buddy to feel secure, knowing he's the child in the household. You, as the parent, need to offer consistent and calm leadership.

"It's about mutual respect and leadership. Buddy needs to understand where he stands in your household. It's fundamental for a healthy relationship between you two. Many of my clients face challenges because they have a skewed relationship with their dog."

I leaned back, processing this revelation. My previous understanding never emphasised the importance of respect or defining roles. And the newer positive training methods seemed to revolve around rewarding dogs with treats rather than strong leadership. Suddenly, everything started to click.

George took the time to guide me through a Leadership Walk and talked me through a few basics. The plan was to start my apprenticeship training Monday morning. Meanwhile, he sent me a series of videos to watch, and suggested that I crate Buddy at night and when I wasn't around. "Since this was so last minute, I figured you wouldn't have time to prepare for Buddy's arrival. I've got a nice crate here for you to use," he said as he pulled one out of his van.

"A crate? Is that really necessary? I mean, he just came from a restrictive cell in the Pound, I don't want him to think that's his life here, too."

George offered a comforting smile, "There are many benefits to crate training. Firstly, we don't know Buddy's toilet habits, especially given he was a backyard dog, previously. Secondly, a crate, when properly introduced, is not a cage, it's a sanctuary. A crate is a cosy den, like his own private bedroom. My dogs voluntarily retreat to their crates when they want some private time. And, thirdly, everything here is new for Buddy. He's being thrust into a vast, unknown space, and that can be overwhelming for a dog. Nervous dogs can be destructive. We want to keep him safe and secure. A strong leader always provides safety and security, crate training is one of those ways."

"The crate is a sacred space for Buddy, not a prison. I hadn't thought of it like that, before." I knelt beside Buddy and gave him a hug. "I'm so grateful, George, thank you!" Buddy licked my cheek and I laughed. "We may have to give you a bath, Buddy, you're stinky."

"I'd hold off on a bath, right now," George cautioned. "Give him time to settle in, to recognise you as his leader, and to trust you, first. You might see it as an act of care, while for Buddy, it's another layer of stress in an already unfamiliar setting. You're still new to him. Let's allow him some time to adjust and build trust."

We set up Buddy's crate in the living room. George showed me how to guide Buddy into the crate and some basic crate training techniques, reminding me to watch those videos for details. We also spoke about food and, since Buddy didn't come with any kibble, I should just start him off with some nice raw mince and watch his bathroom habits.

"Let Buddy relax at home for the next few days," he advised. "Avoid taking him out in public for now. Remember, he has been a backyard dog with very little public experience. I'm going to leave you this slip lead, just in case. We'll fit him for a nice Martingale collar on Monday morning and we'll go over all the protocols for walking and basic training then. Just keep it low key. Everything is new for him and we don't know how he'll react.

"Everything is explained in the videos I sent you. Please take the time to watch them, and let me know if you have any questions. I'll always get back to you as soon as possible. Truly. Text me any time, and I'll see you Monday at my facility."

I walked George out to his van. He pulled out his phone and texted a link to me. "As well as those specific basic videos I sent you, I have given you access to my website at www.DogLeadershipAcademy.com, where you can just ask the system any questions and it will provide you the answers you need, immediately. I have filled it with all my specific dog training knowledge. It's not just a knowledge base, it is fully interactive where you can talk to the system as if you are chatting to me. This way, you can access my videos and processes at any time for specific information without having to sit through hours of videos online or scanning through article after article. It's a great way of finding something fast, especially if I'm unable to answer you if I'm working with a client."

George stepped into his van, lowered the window, and added, "I have a full client schedule this weekend, yet I check my phone regularly. I am here for you, just give me a call or text if you have any questions. We'll dive into your proper training Monday, just go slow with Buddy. Build trust and leadership, and reach out with questions. I'm very happy for you and Buddy."

As George eased down the street, he waved out the window and shouted, "See you Monday!"

I watched George's car disappear down the street and I felt suddenly alone. That was a lot of information. My knees felt a bit wobbly as I realised the responsibility for Buddy's well-being now pressed heavily upon my shoulders. Taking a deep breath, I turned, and walked into the house, toward Buddy. My Buddy.

The kitchen was a mess from our earlier discussions and the preparation of Buddy's meal. I set about tidying up, wiping down the counters and washing the dishes. The rhythmic motion of scrubbing and rinsing was therapeutic, allowing me to process everything George had shared, and repeating it aloud, conversationally, with Buddy, also solidified it in my mind.

The kettle whistled, signalling that the water was to temperature. I brewed myself a cup of lavender tea, hoping it would help calm my nerves. Buddy watched me from the crate with curious eyes, his head tilting slightly as if trying to decipher my every move.

I leaned over, released Buddy, and shuttled him out back to relieve him. He spent some time sniffing the perimeter, and looking into the shrubs before finding a spot to pee. I escorted him inside, grabbed my tea, picked up a book from the coffee table, and settled onto the sofa. Buddy stood before me, with those big brown eyes full of hope. Grinning, I patted the cushion beside me and he eagerly jumped up beside me and nestled into the crook of my arm. With every gentle stroke of his fur and scratch behind his ears, I could feel him relax, his body melting into mine. I relaxed, too, thoroughly enjoying the weight of his head on my lap, his warm breath on my leg was so heart-warming. I cherished this quiet, bonding moment, and I posted several photos of gratitude and joy on several social media platforms and to all my friends.

As the evening wore on, the relaxing tea and cuddles worked their magic and my eyelids grew heavy. The day's events had taken their toll, and I could feel sleep beckoning. Setting the book aside, I stretched and yawned, signalling to Buddy that it was bedtime.

After one final trip to the backyard, I stood by his crate and called, "Come on, Buddy. It's bed time." Buddy was reluctant. He walked back toward the sofa, his eyes pleading for a few more minutes of snuggle time. I tried to be firm, guiding him by the collar toward his crate. He hesitated, yet eventually settled in, albeit with a hint of reluctance.

"Goodnight, Buddy," I whispered, covering him with a soft blanket, and closing the crate door. I shut off the lights and made my way upstairs, hoping for a peaceful night's rest.

As I was on the brink of sleep, Buddy's plaintive howl shattered the quiet. His distress echoed throughout the house, pulling at my heart. I tried to drown out the sound, recalling George's counsel about giving Buddy time to adjust. As the minutes passed, and the howling increased, my anxiety heightened. His plaintive cries tore at my soul and troubled my mind not only for Buddy, but also for the potential disturbance to my neighbours.

Caught in a dilemma between comforting Buddy and maintaining boundaries, I grappled with my decision. In a moment of weakness, I opened his crate and allowed him to roam freely. Almost instantly, Buddy hopped onto the sofa, saving me the corner seat. I heaved a sigh and escorted him back outside to see if there was anything else he needed to do before bed. He poked around a bit, then sat on the patio looking at me.

"Okay, mister, we need some sleep. Let's go to crate." I guided Buddy back to the crate, fluffed his blanket, and shut the door. "Good night, sweet boy. Go to sleep."

The tranquillity was fleeting. Buddy's barking began anew, amplifying my concerns about the neighbours. Torn between his evident unease and my own fatigue, I permitted him to wander the house while I sought refuge in my bedroom, praying for a few hours of undisturbed sleep. We could start fresh tomorrow. I'll watch all those videos and figure out this crate training situation in the morning.

Chapter Summary

In this chapter, we emphasise the profound impact even small donations can have on rescues, advocating for consistent contributions, even if minimal.
Key Concepts:

1. **Supporting Rescues Financially**: Even a donation as small as $1 a week can make a difference. If many individuals contribute, the cumulative effect can be substantial, aiding in saving lives and providing for the dogs' needs.
2. **Promotion through Social Media**: Engaging with rescue posts by liking, commenting, and sharing can amplify their reach. This not only aids in the adoption of dogs but also prevents unnecessary euthanasia by raising awareness.
3. **Avoiding the Pity Trap**: While compassion for rescue dogs is essential, pity can be detrimental. Overindulgence or lack of boundaries due to pity can lead to the Kindness Paradox, where short-term kindness results in long-term behavioural issues.
4. **Establishing Hierarchical Relationships**: It's crucial to define the nature of the relationship with the dog. The dog should understand its place in the family hierarchy, ensuring a functional and harmonious relationship.
5. **Avoiding Dysfunctional Dynamics**: Just as children shouldn't dictate family decisions, dogs, even more so, shouldn't be placed on an equal footing with humans in the household. This ensures balance and mutual respect.

Meet My Behaviourist: Your Personal Dog Training Guide

Are you struggling with your dog's behavior? Whether it's aggressive greetings with guests, excessive barking, or separation anxiety, I've got you covered. I've downloaded hundreds of hours of proven training content into *My Behaviourist*—your go-to tool for personalized, step-by-step dog training solutions.

Here's how it works: simply type your question into *My Behaviourist*, and you'll get clear, actionable advice tailored to your specific situation. Live in an apartment? Your answer will look different from someone with acres of land. Have a large German Shepherd? Your training tips may differ from those for a small Maltese. Every piece of guidance is customized to fit your lifestyle, your dog's breed, and their unique needs.

Let's face it—training doesn't always go as planned. That's where *My Behaviourist* truly shines. You can ask follow-up questions, troubleshoot issues, or request alternative approaches. For example, "I tried that, but it didn't work—what else can I do?" And just like that, *My Behaviourist* will provide fresh ideas to keep you moving forward.

What's the catch? My mission is simple: to empower you with as much information as possible so we can prevent dogs from being surrendered or euthanized due to poor behavior. Far too often, these situations arise from a lack of guidance—not bad dogs or bad owners. I want to change that by giving you the tools you need to succeed.

It's like having me right there with you, every step of the way. And the best part? *My Behaviourist* is completely free. No subscriptions, no credit card required—just reliable, professional advice at your fingertips.

Visit www.dogleadershipacademy.com today and start your journey to a happier, more harmonious relationship with your dog. Let *My Behaviourist* help you bring out the best in your furry baby!

For more resources, guides, videos and personal coaching come to
www.DogLeadershipAcademy.com

Use Phone to Scan QRCode

5

Rewarding For the Right Behaviour

At 6am, Don't Stop Believin' pulled me from sleep. As I threw off the covers, I thought about Buddy waiting for me downstairs. I slipped into yoga pants and a tee, and skipped halfway downstairs before freezing at the tableau before me. Buddy, who had heard me coming, was sitting at the base of the stairs, grinning, tail wagging with happiness. Surrounding Buddy was the heaped and scattered foamy remains of every sofa cushion except the one we had cuddled together on the previous night. The remains of the red cushion covers scattered amidst the white drifts of polyfoam like a murder scene from a Muppet factory. As I absorbed the destruction before me, mouth agape, Buddy sensed I wasn't pleased. His tail stopped wagging and he looked up at me from a bowed head. I descended and sat on the bottom step, invited Buddy over to sit beside me, and gave him pats. I was angry, more so at myself than Buddy. I should have listened to George's advice. Buddy gave me a tentative kiss and the very tip of his tail wiggled back and forth.

"It's my fault, Buddy. Tonight, you absolutely need to sleep in that crate. Meanwhile, let's get you outside while I clean up this mess."

While making breakfast, I watched the crate training video George had sent me. I was supposed to give him something to occupy him in the crate, a bone or a toy. I hadn't had time to buy Buddy any toys. Well, I'd remedy that right after breakfast.

Eager to start working with Buddy and giving Buddy everything that he had missed out on, I decided to walk Buddy the three blocks to the nearest pet store. Supplies were needed, and it was a lovely day. I reviewed the Leadership Walk I'd learned briefly yesterday as I grabbed my purse and keys. I had just locked the door behind me when Buddy shot forward, tugging me down the walk, through the gate, and along the sidewalk. I was definitely not in control. Buddy's strength was overwhelming, dragging me haphazardly down the street.

The world rushed past in a blur as I struggled to maintain my footing. My heart pounded in my chest, each beat matching the rhythm of Buddy's eager strides. The smell of fresh morning air mixed with the earthy scent of Buddy's fur, and the rough texture of the leash chafed against my skin. I had seen countless YouTube videos extolling the benefits of dog walks for mental stimulation and enrichment. But this chaos? This was exhausting...and dangerous.

I eventually got us turned around and on the right path to the pet store. I arrived sweaty and flustered. The kind shop assistant suggested a high-quality harness instead of a collar. He argued that collars could be harmful and that a good harness would help me manage Buddy better, and it was the best solution for safe riding in cars. Despite the hefty price tag, I decided to give it a shot for Buddy's sake. A small fortune in equipment, toys, and treats later, Buddy and I set out for home. Despite our frantic pace there, the trip home was no easier. If anything, Buddy pulled harder and I had no control over him as I jogged to keep pace. We were almost home when a nearby car backfired. The loud bang frightened Buddy. In his panic, he jerked back and slipped out of the harness. I watched in horror as he flew past me. Buddy was a blur of fur and energy as he darted into traffic, narrowly missing a car not once, but twice. My heart pounded in my chest as I desperately tried to catch him. The taste of fear was bitter in my mouth, and my hands trembled.

Thankfully, I managed to grab Buddy behind a neighbour's hedge. He was safe, but I was an emotional wreck. Holding onto his collar, we squat-walked back to the house. Once inside, I slammed and locked the door behind us. My legs gave out, and I slid down the door, ending up in a heap on the entryway tiles.

"How could I be so stupid?!" I berated myself. The staff at the pound had mentioned that Buddy had spent most of his life in a backyard. He likely hadn't experienced much of the outside world. Yet, in my eagerness to provide him with new experiences, I'd overwhelmed him with unfamiliar stimuli. It was no wonder he'd bolted. Poor Buddy. I needed to remember George's teachings. I had to be a parent to Buddy. As a parent, my role wasn't just to provide for him but also to protect, advocate, and set him up for success.

Buddy, now much calmer and seemingly oblivious to my internal turmoil, decided the floor was as good a place as any to cuddle. He nestled into the crook of my arm, soon drifting off to sleep. As I waited for my heart rate to return to normal and feeling to come back to my legs, I realised that our walk had been anything but the enriching experience I had hoped for.

I looked down at my sleeping Buddy, and I began to question myself. Doubt seeped in, whispers of insecurity in my mum's voice had me questioning my ability to manage this. "Can I really do this? Was I wrong to think I could handle a rescue dog?" I swallowed the lump of anxiety forming in my throat, picked myself up from the floor – quite literally – and flopped onto the one remaining sofa cushion with a glass of water. Buddy joined me almost immediately.

In need of a reassuring voice, I called Sally. After a couple of rings, she answered with her usual cheer, "Hey Em, what's up?"

I didn't bother hiding my distress. "Sally, I…I don't know if I can do this. Buddy…he's just…he's a lot," I admitted, my voice quivering with frustration. "I keep hearing my mum's dire warnings in my head… I almost lost him on a walk just now. He could have died. I screwed up. Big time," I sobbed.

Sally paused, allowing me to catch my breath. "Em, I get it," she finally said. "But if you give up on Buddy now, he won't have a chance. And your mum…you know how she can be. If you quit, you're just proving her right. Buddy is counting on you."

We chatted on speaker while I hugged Buddy close to me. Sally reminded me how hard I'd worked to manifest Buddy in my life, that she trusted my ability to figure it all out and become an amazing dog behaviourist. "Besides," she said with a smile in her voice, "You can't give up, you need to figure all this out and teach me how to handle Benji! You're going to be my Obi-Wan!"

"You're right, Sally," I laughed at her geeky reference. "I can't give up. Not on Buddy. And definitely not because of mum." With renewed resolve, I braced myself for the challenges ahead. I was in this for the long run, for both Buddy and myself.

I took advantage of the sleepy Buddy cuddle to watch the crate training video George had sent me for a second time, then I escorted him outside while I prepped dinner and sorted through all the loot from the pet store. I set out a nice raised food and water bowl set, opened a bag of treats into a nice clip jar to keep them fresh, and kept one nice bone aside for crate entertainment tonight.

Well before bedtime, I began Buddy's crate training. I gently directed Buddy to his crate. He stepped in hesitantly, eyeing me to check if it was an option. I was resolute. No options. I placed the bone in the crate with Buddy and latched the door, then I stepped back, leaving Buddy to settle in his new space.

After watching several of George's videos and typing specific questions into his website at www.DogLeadershipAcademy.com, I was able to drill down, ask clarifying questions on points that still confused me. The system was surprisingly intuitive and helpful, as if I was interacting with George directly. I had a plan.

The strategy George suggested was **counter conditioning** and **positive association techniques** to help Buddy see the crate as a positive space rather than a prison. The goal was to make Buddy associate the crate with good things. My plan was to reward his quiet, calm behaviour in the crate with treats, praise, and freedom. This would gradually build this positive connection.

As I watched, Buddy was completely engrossed with his bone. I observed Buddy closely, trying to gauge his reactions. Just before he looked like he was getting tired of the bone, I opened the door to allow him out. The plan was to release Buddy before he felt trapped or anxious. I wanted him to learn that staying calm meant freedom, and that barking wasn't going to garner the results he wanted.

We practiced this repeatedly. Sometimes, Buddy started barking as soon as the door shut, even before I could open it. Instead of reacting to his barks, I stepped back and waited until he was quiet, sending the clear message that barking doesn't open the door.

After numerous training sessions, Buddy began to get it. He'd enter the crate, stay silent, and exit without any fuss. It was a slow process that demanded a lot of patience from me, but each small win boosted my confidence. The crate transformed from a source of anxiety to a place associated with peace and rewards. This was a huge step forward for both of us.

Through this training, I realised that the previous night, I had unintentionally been rewarding Buddy for barking. Every time he barked in the crate, I let him out, anxious about bothering my neighbours. This taught Buddy that barking meant freedom. Once I changed my approach, Buddy learned that the rewards came when he was calm and silent.

As we continued to practice, it became a game. I'd command, "Buddy, crate." Buddy would enter, turn, and sit watching me. Sometimes I'd close the gate, walk away, and return to find him curled up on his plush blanket. Sometimes, he was still sitting there waiting for me to reenter the room. I asked, "Do you want to come out?" He stared at me with those big brown eyes and stomped his two front paws. I opened the gate and give him all kinds of cuddles and love.

My next project was back door training. I told Buddy to go outside, and then closed the door behind him. If Buddy stayed quiet, I'd open the door as a reward. If he barked, the door stayed shut. I had to act before Buddy got too anxious, opening the door while he was still calm to prevent barking.

It was challenging and required a lot of patience and determination on my part, yet I was committed. As Buddy began to understand, I saw the results – a quiet, calm Buddy who knew barking wasn't the answer. This was a huge achievement for both of us.

When it was time for dinner, I fed Buddy in the crate, associating it further with comfort and a place for good things to happen to him. Every meal in the crate reinforced its positive nature. I also rewarded Buddy with treats when he was quiet in the crate, showing him that his calm behaviour was valued. If he barked, I ignored him, signalling that barking wasn't a winning practice.

My method was all about positive reinforcement. I rewarded the behaviours I wanted and ignored the ones I didn't. Over the hours, Buddy caught on, leading to a more peaceful coexistence.

When it was time to retire, I let Buddy out one more time, then told him to go to crate. I told him he was a very good boy and I'd see him in the morning. To my delight, Buddy settled quietly in his crate. The house was filled with a blissful silence, and my remaining sofa cushion was safe.

In bed, I reflected on the day. It had started chaotically, with Buddy dragging me everywhere, yet it ended with Buddy peacefully in his crate. I realised the importance of what I'd accomplished. I'd found a way to teach Buddy to be quiet in the crate, rewarding his silence and ignoring his barks.

I was tingling with pride. I faced a challenge and came out on top. The silence of the night was punctuated by Buddy's occasional snores. He was comfortably sleeping in his crate. I grinned as I realised that I could do this. I was ready to face the challenges of training Buddy and learning how to train others. Patience, positive reinforcement, and strong leadership were the keys. It was a win and, more importantly, a promising beginning to our journey together.

Chapter Summary

In this chapter, we delve into essential equipment and training tips for dog owners. We discuss the importance of selecting the right walking equipment, emphasising the potential pitfalls of certain popular choices. The chapter also introduces the concept of crate training, highlighting its benefits and methods to make it a positive experience for dogs. Additionally, we touch upon the significance of understanding and managing barking behaviour and the importance of training dogs under their stress threshold.

Key Concepts:

1. **Crate Training**: The crate is portrayed as a sanctuary for dogs, akin to a private room for teenagers. Positive associations, like placing treats, activities, or feeding the dog inside the crate can make it a pleasant space for the dog. Crates also serve as protective measures against potential accidents or property damage.
2. **Managing Barking**: Owners are advised to be mindful of the behaviours they reward. If barking is inadvertently rewarded, it reinforces the behaviour. It's essential to reward desired behaviours and not unintentionally encourage unwanted ones.
3. **Training Under Threshold**: The chapter emphasises the importance of training dogs under their stress threshold to ensure they are not overwhelmed, promoting effective and positive learning experiences.
4. **Proper Equipment**: A martingale collar and slip lead are the best ways of controlling a dog and preventing them from tugging out of regular collars and harnesses.

Get Your Free Companion Workbook!

Download the *Beyond Treats Companion Workbook* for practical, step-by-step exercises, daily training guides, and self-assessment tools to help you transform your relationship with your dog. Visit www.dogleadershipacademy.com to get your free copy today!

6

Marker Training and the Dog Park

The next morning, I woke filled with a fresh sense of excitement. I was keen to continue working with Buddy on our training exercises. After letting him out in the backyard for his usual morning activities, we headed back inside for coffee and to watch the next set of George's videos.

I watched George introduce the concept of marker training. Marker training, frequently referred to as clicker training, is a foundational technique in dog training. I grabbed a notepad and took some essential notes for myself.

1. **Identification of Desired Behaviour:** The primary objective of marker training is to clearly and instantly communicate to Buddy when he has performed a desired behaviour. This immediate feedback helps Buddy understand exactly what action earned a reward. For example, asking Buddy to sit and marking his success.
2. **Use of a Marker:** The marker is a distinct and consistent signal, like YES! Every time Buddy performs the desired behaviour, this signal is IMMEDIATELY GIVEN, with enthusiasm. Over time, Buddy begins to associate the marker with having done something correctly.
3. **Reward:** After the marker is given, Buddy is promptly rewarded, with a treat, toy and/or lavish praises. This reinforces the positive behaviour, making it more likely Buddy will repeat it in the future.

MARKER TRAINING AND THE DOG PARK

While some trainers use the clicker as a tool for marker training due to its unique sound, it's not the only option. I discovered that trainers, like George Tran, prefer using verbal markers. Verbal markers have the advantage of always being available since you don't need a physical tool, and they can be more personal and flexible.

I recalled George's training session with Buddy the other day, and I remembered how effectively he used the word YES as his marker. Inspired by his approach, I felt a natural inclination to adopt Yes with Buddy. It seemed more intuitive to me, and I was confident that it would resonate with Buddy, helping him understand and respond positively.

I integrated marker training into our crate sessions. I told Buddy to go to crate, then watched him closely. At the precise moment he settled quietly in the crate, I enthusiastically said Yes. Following the marker, I showered him with words of praise and offered him a treat as a reward. This tied his action, the verbal marker, and praise together for him.

The last step in our new routine was releasing Buddy from the crate. I did this right after giving him the treat, offering him another layer of positive reinforcement for his calm behaviour. The process was straightforward and impactful. It identified the behaviour I expected of him, rewarded it instantly, and then strengthened it with something Buddy cherished - freedom from the crate and physical attention.

I was making Buddy's breakfast when my phone chirped. Sally's face appeared on my screen. I hit the green dot and greeted my dear friend. Sally was crying. She was at the vet's office. Benji was in surgery after he was attacked in the dog park this morning.

"Hang on, Sally, I'll be right there!" I finished Buddy's breakfast, fed him in the crate, closed the crate door and then grabbed my wallet, and dashed out the door promising him I'd be back as soon as possible.

In the clinic, Sally was curled into a chair, hugging her knees. I ran over and wrapped my arms around her. "Oh, Sally, I'm here. What happened?" Through tears and sobs, Sally told me of her morning.

As Sally recounted the incident, I saw the dog park scene unfolding before my eyes. It was a beautiful morning, and the park was brimming with the joyous energy of dogs running, fetching, and playing. Amidst this beautiful chaos, a disaster loomed.

A new face had joined the park that day, a rescue dog, nervous and unsure. His owner, a well-intentioned yet naive man, had hoped that the dog park would serve as a perfect place for his new companion to learn social skills.

Benji, with his usual friendly vigour, approached the newcomer. The man watched, hopeful that this could be the start of his pet's socialisation journey, as things took a tragic turn. The rescue dog, unsocialized and fearful, lashed out at Benji. The joyful atmosphere became a scene of panic.

The man was horrified! He grabbed his dog, pulling him off Benji wondering how this could have gone so terribly wrong so incredibly quickly. Guilt washed over him as he realised the consequences of his ill-informed decision to allow his new rescue off leash in public. The sight of poor Benji, bleeding on the ground, was a stark contrast to the playful pup he had seen running around just moments ago.

Sally had grabbed Benji and raced to the clinic, they had taken him into surgery immediately. We waited together, holding hands, for the vet to emerge. When he did, he assured Sally that Benji was going to be fine. The physical damage he had sustained would all heal in time, yet she would need to work with a behaviourist if Benji became fearful of other dogs after this.

"I see this all too often," the vet explained in a sombre tone. "Dog parks can be great, but they can also be dangerous for untrained or unstable dogs. All too often, owners bring their pets in hopes of socialising them without proper training and they don't think to keep a leash on them. A dog park is a largely unsupervised playground. Pet parents need to be alert and proactive. If you see a potential danger – be it a bully or a dog displaying aggressive behaviour – you should take action, or take your dog and leave the park. It's a good idea to keep a new dog on a leash until you're certain of their behaviour. Also, many professional trainers and behaviourists advise their clients to consider private playdates for pets, much like you would for your children. This way, you know who your pet is interacting with, and you can control the environment to better ensure safety."

His advice struck a chord, reminding us of our responsibility as pet owners.

The dog park wasn't just a playground; it was a place that demanded our attention and vigilance. The responsibility of ensuring our pets' safety was in our hands.

A chill traversed my spine. That tragedy could have happened to Buddy. We were still working to establish trust, Buddy could have been the attacker. The Pound had said he had a history of aggression toward other dogs, what if I had been foolish enough to take him to a dog park? I shuddered.

The vet discussed post operative treatment and how to keep Benji comfortable while he healed with Sally. As they finished at the counter, I thanked my lucky stars I had chosen to focus on Buddy's training before throwing him into the social mix. The stark realisation solidified my determination to help Buddy overcome his behavioural issues and learn how to teach others to help their dogs. It also served as a reminder of the responsibility that came with being a pet parent – it was not just about giving love and treats, it was also about understanding and guiding our furry companions toward well-adjusted happiness.

Chapter Summary

In this chapter, we introduce the concept of using a compliance marker in dog training and provide valuable strategies for navigating dog parks. We emphasise the importance of creating positive associations for dogs and ensuring their safety and well-being in public spaces.

Key Concepts:

1. **Compliance Marker**: The chapter introduces the idea of front-loading your dog by training them to associate the word YES with approval and rewards. In the initial stages, simple commands like "sit" should be immediately followed by a YES, and then treats and/or praises. This helps the dog understand that YES signifies reward, love, and approval.
2. **Dog Park Tips**: The chapter offers several strategies for ensuring a

positive experience at dog parks:

- - Timing: Opt for less busy times to avoid potential encounters with unstable dogs brought in by unaware owners.
- - Pro activity: If an aggressive or bullying dog is spotted, it's advised to leave the park to avoid confrontations.
- - Advocacy: Owners should stand up for their dogs and ensure they aren't subjected to bullying from other dogs.
- - Fearful Dogs: It's recommended to avoid bringing fearful dogs to the park, as they can become targets for attacks due to the inherent nature of dogs lacking morality. Dogs in a group can target fearful dogs much like bullies in a playground.

For more information on marker training and the ability to ask any dog questions directly through our system that has been programmed with hundreds of hours of content from George, come to www.DogLeadershipAcademy.com.

Ready for More In-Depth Guidance?

If you're looking for a deeper dive into the principles and strategies discussed in this chapter, don't forget to download your free copy of the **Dog Leadership Training Guide** at **www.dogleadershipacademy.com**.

This comprehensive guide offers:

- **Detailed Summaries:** Clear, structured explanations of key concepts.
- **Step-by-Step Instructions:** Practical, easy-to-follow exercises to implement leadership-based training.
- **Expanded Insights:** Understand the *why* behind every method to build confidence in your approach.

Download it today and take the next step toward becoming the calm, consistent leader your dog respects and trusts. **Visit www.dogleadershipacademy.com now!**

7

Leadership Based Training

The morning sun cast a warm, golden hue as I stepped out of my house, the scent of blooming jasmine wafted through the air. Today was the day: my first training session with George at his facility. Anticipation bubbled inside me, a mix of excitement and nervousness. Buddy, reading my energy, danced beside me as I prepared the back seat for him.

   I guided him into the back of the car and secured him with a harness that clicked into the seat belt. His tail beat a rapid rhythm against the seat and I felt his breath panting into my neck as I ensured he was safely strapped in. I took his face in my hands, stared into his eyes and asked, "Are you ready for a new adventure?" Buddy stomped his front paws in answer.

   I started the car, set the GPS, hit shuffle on my favourite classic rock playlist, and we turned onto the road. The journey to George's facility was filled with a whirlwind of emotions.

   "What if I can't do this?"

   "What if George thinks I'm not cut out for this?"

   The demon of self-doubt sparred with the confident cheerleader in my head. To tamp both of them into the background, I cranked the volume of my music and found myself singing along to Bon Jovi's song, It's My Life.

   This is my life, I affirmed. I didn't like where it was going and I manifested this opportunity to change. If I had failed, Buddy would be dead, pure and simple. Grateful that I was on my way to learn how to become the best leader possible for Buddy, and that I was going to do my best to turn that into a new career for myself, my resolve hardened. The stakes were too high, I had to succeed.

The city faded into fields and forests, and the air was fresh and clean as Buddy and I arrived at George's facility. I rang George and he met me at the gate with a beautiful border collie. Buddy, still harnessed in the back seat, growled low at the sight of the black and white dog. Despite Buddy's behaviour, the collie was alert, yet remained obediently by George's side.

"Welcome to Gracie's Haven," George announced. Glancing at the eager border collie, he added, "Meet Gracie. She's the star of our facility, and we've named this place in her honour."

"First thing, first. We need to give you a bit of a tour and orientation, and we want Buddy to be safe while we do so. Gracie," he turned to the collie, "go home." Gracie trotted off through the back fence. George turned back to me, "Because we have so many dogs on site, I'm going to handle Buddy. We have an enclosure ready for him where he can relax while we settle you in." He pulled a slip lead from his pocket, and led us both into the facility.

Once Buddy was secure in a nice shady spot, George inquired, genuine concern in his voice, "How have you and Buddy been, Emily? I haven't heard from you, so I'm hoping all has been well."

I took a deep breath and talked about Buddy's behaviour and all that happened over the weekend. "Your videos and website (www.DogLeadershipAcademy.com) have been really helpful. I've been diving into marker training on my own, and I've been working with Buddy on crate training. I think I'd have gone mad without your guidance."

A proud smile stretched across George's face. "That's awesome, Emily. I'm sorry I couldn't be around earlier. There is always so much to do and so many people to help." He paused, "Are you ready to learn some more tools to help you with Buddy?"

I nodded eagerly. George gestured for me to follow him, and we stepped into the facility. The sound of dogs barking and playing filled the air. As we walked, George began to share the stories of the dogs that called this facility home. As I listened, I felt a deep sense of respect for the man before me. His passion was tangible, and his dedication to saving lives was evident in every word.

He stopped in front of an enclosure where a beautiful kelpie/rottweiler mix named Shadow was playing. Her sleek black coat glistened in the sun, and her eyes sparkled with mischief. "This is Shadow," George began, his voice filled with pride. "She was scheduled to be euthanized after she attacked a small dog. No rescue would take her, but look at her now. She's not only a part of our pack, she's also a trainer dog. She helps less socialised dogs learn to be calm and less fearful."

We continued our tour, and George introduced me to Fluffy, a massive black German shepherd with a commanding presence. Despite his size, there was a gentleness in his eyes. "Fluffy had human aggression issues due to his anxiety and fear of abandonment," George explained. "With time, patience, and training, he's now an integral part of our team, helping other dogs learn proper etiquette."

Each dog had a story, a past filled with pain and trauma, yet here, they were given a second chance. A chance to heal, to grow, and to thrive.

As we walked, I turned to George, gestured to the facility around us and inquired, "Why are you doing this?"

George paused, taking a deep breath. "I've had other businesses before this," he began, his voice filled with emotion, "And they were fine, yet I couldn't stand by and watch these dogs suffer and die when I could make a difference. It started small, just my wife and I fostering dogs and rehoming them. Soon, it became my passion to give these dogs a second chance."

His words resonated deeply with me. The power of hope and compassion was evident in every corner of the facility. It was the driving force behind George's mission and the foundation of his success.

George's eyes twinkled as he looked at me. "Do you want to know the secret sauce of our magic here?" he asked with a playful grin.

I nodded eagerly.

"Hang in there, we'll circle back to that and it'll make sense," he teased.

"One of my key requirements for all my apprentices is that they actively support rescue groups. Rescues are the unsung heroes of the dog world, stepping in to pick up the pieces when humans fail. While many people turn to these organizations when they need to rehome their dogs, few offer help when rescues need financial support. Vet bills, food, and other expenses aren't cheap or free, and these organizations often struggle to make ends meet. That's why it's vital for my students to not only help with the most challenging cases but also to promote these dogs by posting bios, sharing glamour shots, and spreading the word to find them loving homes. Supporting rescues in this way ensures we're giving back to those who work tirelessly to save dogs in need."

As I listened to George, I felt a renewed sense of purpose. I was here to make a difference, to be a beacon of hope for these dogs, and to carry forward George's legacy of compassion and hope.

"Emily," he began, his voice soft yet firm, "every dog that comes through those gates, no matter their past, no matter the mistakes or sins they may have committed, they get a fresh start here. We don't judge them based on their past. We see them for who they can become, not who they once were."

I looked around, taking in the sight of dogs playing, training, and resting. Each one had a story, a history, yet here, they were given a new narrative. A narrative of hope, love, and redemption.

George continued, "Our secret sauce, Emily, is simple. It's dignity and compassion. We treat every dog that comes to us with the respect and love they deserve. We don't see them as broken or damaged, we see them as souls in need of understanding and care."

He gestured toward a section of the facility where a group of dogs was playing. "Once they've been rehabilitated, once they've learned to trust and love again, we don't just stop there. We house them, care for them, and most importantly, we help find them loving homes. Homes where they will be cherished, where their past will be just that… a past."

I felt a warmth spread through me as I listened to George. His words, his mission, it was all so pure and genuine. It was evident that this wasn't just a job for him; it was a calling.

"We believe in second chances here, Emily," George concluded, his eyes filled with a fierce determination. "Every dog deserves a chance at a better life, and we're here to give every one of them the best possible chance to do so."

I took in the facility as a whole. "George, this is all incredible, but where does the money come from to fund all of this?"

George leaned back, a thoughtful expression on his face. "Emily, I've never been a fan of begging people for money. I believe in a fair exchange—providing value and receiving value in return."

He gestured around the facility. "I dedicate my time to helping people with their dogs' behaviour problems. Through DogLeadershipAcademy.com, we offer practical solutions that people are willing to pay for because they see the value in transforming their dogs' lives. The proceeds from that work go directly into funding this facility, paying the staff, covering the rent, buying food, and everything else needed to keep this place running."

George's eyes softened as he continued, "But it doesn't stop there. A portion of the profits from this book and DogLeadershipAcademy.com also goes to supporting other rescues. These rescues are always underfunded and struggling, and by helping people with their dogs, we can give back even more. Every dollar we earn not only helps solve behaviour issues but also contributes to saving more dogs from being surrendered or euthanised."

He leaned forward, his voice earnest as we continued our tour. "Emily, our training philosophy at DogLeadershipAcademy.com is rooted in leadership and respect. While treats have their place, they aren't the be-all and end-all. There are other, more effective methods, and by teaching these, we're able to make a real difference—for the dogs, their owners, and for the countless dogs out there waiting for a second chance."

"Some trainers," George began with a hint of disdain, "resort to dominance-based training. It's a method that relies on violence, threats, and cruelty to force a dog into submission. It's akin to those parents who believe in ruling with an iron fist and physical abuse. Yes, it might produce results, but at what cost? It's inhumane, and there are far better ways."

I nodded, processing his words. "So, where does treat based training fit into the spectrum?"

George paused, observed a group of dogs napping together in the shade as he gathered his thoughts. "Emily, at their core, dogs are predators with deeply ingrained primal urges. While we've domesticated them over thousands of years, these instincts remain. There are moments when a treat simply won't override a dog's natural drive, no matter what some trainers might suggest. In other words, what I am saying is that while treats are great for training new behaviours, dogs also need to be told what not to do."

I leaned in, intrigued. "So, you're saying that there are situations where just offering a treat won't work?"

He nodded, "Exactly. Think of it this way, if a child were drawing on a wall and you only handed them a drawing book with praise when they used it, they might never understand that drawing on the wall was inappropriate in the first place."

I pondered on this, trying to connect the dots. "So, in essence, by relying solely on positive reinforcement, we're missing out on teaching them about consequences?"

"Yes, Emily, yet it goes deeper than that. While every trainer has their unique approach to training, there's a significant issue I've observed with the treat only method. When these trainers encounter dogs with deeply ingrained or uncontrollable primal urges, and they can't redirect these behaviours using just treats, they often label the dog as 'untrainable.'"

I frowned, "And what happens to these 'untrainable' dogs?"

George's eyes darkened, and his voice held a hint of anger. "That's the heartbreaking part. I have encountered many stories from my clients that these trainers would often recommend euthanasia."

I felt a lump forming in my throat and immediately thought of how close Buddy came to dying. "So, they'd rather end a life than try a different approach?"

George nodded, his passion evident. "That's precisely why I'm so fervent about leadership-based training. It's not about dominance; it's about understanding, respect, and guidance. When training fails, it's not just a matter of a dog misbehaving. In many cases, dogs lose their lives. We owe it to them to explore every possible avenue to help them adjust and thrive."

"So, tell me about your **leadership-based training**, why is it different?"

George smiled, a glimmer of hope in his eyes. "Leadership-based training is about guiding our dogs, setting clear expectations, and helping them understand their place in our world. It's about what not to do as well as what to do. <u>Much like a parent teaching and guiding their child.</u>"

George leaned against a fence, "Leadership-based training is about mutual respect. It's about guiding the dog, setting expectations, and establishing a relationship built on trust. It's not about dominance, it's about understanding and communication. Leadership training is all about clarity and establishing, without a shadow of a doubt, the nature of the relationship between the parent and the dog."

He paused, allowing his words to sink in. "Imagine a household where children have an equal say in every decision, from finances to bedtime. It would be chaotic, right?"

I nodded, picturing the mayhem that would ensue having children insist on having ice-cream for dinner every night.

George continued, "What's even more concerning is that many families, without realising it, defer to their dogs. They let the dog dictate the rules of the house. It might sound absurd, but it's more common than you'd think.

"Think about it, Emily. What kind of a household would it be if the dog decides when it's time for a walk, barking and demanding attention? Where mealtimes are dictated by the dog's whines and nudges? And, when asked to go outside or move off the couch, the dog simply refuses, or worse yet, growling and showing aggressive behaviour?"

I thought about Buddy and some of his behaviours. While he wasn't as demanding, there were moments when he seemed to be testing the boundaries.

George's voice brought me back. "Now, imagine if you behaved this way in your house when you were younger. How would your mother have reacted?"

A shiver ran down my spine as memories of my strict upbringing surfaced. My mother was a formidable woman, one who believed in the adage, 'my house, my rules.' There was no room for negotiation. "I wouldn't have dared," I admitted. "My mother was very clear about boundaries."

George nodded, a knowing smile playing on his lips. "And what if she had

LEADERSHIP BASED TRAINING

let you walk all over her? If she had bent to your every whim and demand?"

The very idea seemed ludicrous. "It would have been a disaster," I confessed. "I might have enjoyed the short-term freedom, but in the long run, I'd have become entitled, spoiled, and probably quite lost."

"That," George said, pointing a finger in the air for emphasis, "is what I call the Kindness Paradox. Parents, in their well-intentioned desire to make their children or dogs happy, avoid being firm. They mistake indulgence for kindness. In reality, this lack of boundaries and discipline often leads to long-term negative consequences."

He leaned back, again. "True kindness, Emily, is providing structure, providing guidance, teaching respect and consequences. It's about preparing them for the world, not shielding them from it."

I absorbed his words, and realised the depth of the lesson. It wasn't just about training Buddy; it was a philosophy that applied to all relationships, whether with pets or people. The Kindness Paradox was a profound insight, one that would shape my approach, not just with Buddy, in all aspects of life.

As George spoke, memories of my childhood flooded my mind. Even though I was adopted, my mother never treated me any differently from her biological children. She was a pillar of strength, a beacon of fairness, and the embodiment of unwavering love. Her parenting style was a blend of strictness and compassion, always firm yet fair.

I remembered the countless times I'd tried to test her boundaries, hoping for an inch of leniency. She never wavered. There were rules, and they were to be followed – not out of fear, but out of respect. She had never resorted to force or violence. Instead, she believed in healthy doses of consequences. If I stepped out of line, there were repercussions, always fitting the misdeed. It wasn't about punishment; it was about understanding the impact of my actions and learning from them.

Her approach wasn't just about maintaining order; it was about instilling values. She taught me responsibility, accountability, and the importance of integrity. Every lesson, every consequence, was a building block in shaping my character.

Then, it suddenly clicked. **The foundation of effective dog training was**

exactly like good parenting—it's about teaching respect, not simply obedience. It's about preparing dogs for life by helping them understand boundaries and consequences. This wasn't about dominance or trick-based obedience; it was about mutual respect, learning, and growth. Just as children look to their parents for guidance, dogs look to their owners. They seek direction, understanding, and most importantly, a sense of belonging and security.

I looked at George, my eyes widening with a new sense of clarity. "It's all starting to make sense now. **Training Buddy isn't just about teaching him commands or getting him to obey.** It's about building a relationship based on trust and respect. It's like the bond I have with my mother."

George nodded, his expression serious yet approving. "Exactly, Emily. Leadership isn't about control; it's about guiding and preparing Buddy for the world around him, just as your mother did for you. And a key part of that guidance is helping Buddy understand that his actions have consequences—just as yours did when you were growing up."

He paused, leaning in to make his point. "Life is full of consequences, Emily. If we put our hand on a hot stove, we get burned. That burn is a reminder—a consequence that teaches us to be careful. In the same way, our job as leaders, whether as parents or as dog owners, is to **expose our children and dogs to controlled consequences**. These small exposures help them grow and become resilient. When they experience challenges, they don't become overwhelmed or reactive because **they understand the world isn't always nice and safe**. They've learned that some actions lead to discomfort or frustration, but they've also learned how to handle it."

I nodded slowly, letting it sink in. "That's what's missing in treat-only training, isn't it? It avoids discomfort at all costs, so the dog never learns that certain behaviours lead to consequences. Without those lessons, they can become reactive, demanding, or anxious because they've never learned to cope with limits."

"Exactly," George continued. "We're seeing a global rise in dogs with behavioural issues because they're often not taught about consequences. Just like children who grow up without boundaries or any exposure to consequences, they become entitled, easily triggered, and reactive. Real leadership, the kind that prepares dogs and children for life, involves helping them understand and work through challenges. By doing this, you're not just creating obedience—you're building resilience, trust, and a lasting bond."

In that moment, I realized that training Buddy wasn't just about him; it was a lesson in leadership and life itself. **True kindness, I now understood, means teaching both love, consequences and limits.**

"So, how do I get Buddy to respect me?" I asked, eager to absorb more of George's wisdom.

George's eyes twinkled, reminiscent of a kung-fu master imparting age-old secrets to an eager young grasshopper. **"The quickest and most effective way to teach a dog leadership, consequences and respect,"** he paused for effect, **"is through the Leadership Walk."**

I blinked in surprise, recalling our first meeting. "You mean like the walk you did with Buddy the first day you brought him to my home? That crazy leash dance you did with him?" I remembered how George had handled Buddy with such confidence and ease, guiding him with gentle corrections and clear intentions, though they hadn't been at all clear to me at the time.

"Exactly," George confirmed with a nod. "The Leadership Walk is more than just a physical activity. It's a dance of communication between you and your dog. It's where you set the tone, establish boundaries, and communicate your expectations. When done correctly, it's a powerful tool to establish your role as a leader."

He continued, "During the walk, you're not just guiding Buddy's movements; you're also guiding his mind. You're teaching him to focus on you, to follow your lead, and to trust your decisions. It's a time for you to be present, assertive, and calm. And in return, Buddy will learn to respect and trust your guidance. In simple terms, '**a leader leads, and a follower follows**.'" George goes on to explain that when most people take their dogs out for a walk, what actually happens is that the dog takes the owners for a walk (more specifically a drag). To establish leadership and respect, the owner should be leading the dog, not the other way around.

As George spoke about the Leadership Walk, I couldn't help but contrast it with my recent experience with Buddy. "George," I began, a hint of embarrassment in my voice, "just the other day, Buddy dragged me all over the place. I felt like a rag doll being tossed around. It was nothing like the Leadership Walk you describe."

George chuckled, his laughter warm and infectious, "Well, every journey has its bumps. There's no time to start like the present. Let's get to it, shall we?"

I followed George back into the main yard. "Before we begin, let me introduce you to Andrew, my assistant. He'll be your primary trainer."

Following George's gaze, my eyes landed on a man who seemed to have walked straight out of a romance novel. Andrew had rugged good looks, a chiselled jawline, and sun-kissed skin that hinted at long hours spent outdoors. He had the build of a country boy, well-muscled, yet not overly so, indicating a life of hard work rather than hours spent in a gym. His attire was simple, a pair of worn, faded jeans and a fitted t-shirt that accentuated his physique.

It was his eyes, though, that truly captivated me. They were a deep shade of blue, intense and piercing, as if they could see right through to my soul. I felt an involuntary shiver run down my spine and I quickly tried to compose myself, hoping my reaction wasn't too evident.

"Emily, meet Andrew," George said, breaking the moment.

I extended my hand and tried to appear casual. "Nice to meet you, Andrew."

Andrew's intense gaze met mine. He took my hand, his grip firm, and gave a curt nod. There was a hint of condescension, as if he had already sized me up and found me lacking.

Determined to prove him wrong, I squared my shoulders and met his intensity head-on. George, sensing the tension, clapped his hands together. "Alright then, let's get started!" he announced, effectively breaking the ice and setting the stage for the training ahead.

Chapter Summary

In this chapter, we delve into the contrasting approaches of dominance-based training and leadership-based training in dog behaviour methodology. We highlight the differences between the two and emphasise the importance of adopting a nurturing and guiding role, akin to that of a parent, in training dogs.

Key Concepts:

1. **Dominance-Based Training**: This method relies on using fear, threats, and even violence to achieve compliance from the dog. It is likened to abusive parenting and is discouraged due to its negative implications on the dog's mental well-being.
2. **Leadership-Based Training**: This approach is rooted in the principles of good leadership:

- Guidance: Leaders provide clear directions, especially in challenging situations, ensuring that the dog knows what is expected.
- Protection and Advocacy: Just as parents protect and advocate for their children, leaders ensure the safety and well-being of their dogs, shielding them from potential harm and standing up for their rights.
- Avoiding Entitlement: Using the parent/child model ensures that dogs do not develop a sense of entitlement, preventing them from making undue demands.

Get Your Free Companion Workbook!

Download the *Beyond Treats Companion Workbook* and get practical step-by-step exercises, self-assessment tools, and detailed templates outlining exactly what to do on Day 1, Day 2, and beyond. Start transforming your relationship with your dog today—visit www.dogleadershipacademy.com to claim your free copy!

8

The Leadership Walk

George asked Andrew to fetch Buddy, then turned to me. "You know," he began, pulling is a learned behaviour. Buddy, with his strength, has figured out that when he pulls, he gets his handler to move forward. It's a success strategy."

I frowned, trying to process his words. "Success strategy, what do you mean?"

He nodded, a hint of amusement in his eyes. "Think about it. In life, when something works for us, we tend to do more of it. Like when a child cries and gets candy, they'll cry more. Or if someone finds that by being a bully, they get their way, which teaches them that bullying is a success strategy for them, so they continue that behaviour. Success strategies are behaviours that have been reinforced because they produce a desired outcome."

I pondered his words, thinking about Buddy's behaviour over the weekend. He barked and was rewarded for his barking when I had let him out that first night. Once we worked to show that quiet behaviour was his new success strategy, he spent the next night content and peaceful.

"So, you're saying Buddy pulls because it's always worked for him." I stated.

"Exactly, and our job is to retrain that belief system. Today, we're going to teach him that pulling gets him nowhere."

"But he's so strong," I protested, recalling the helplessness I'd felt as Buddy had dragged me along. "How can I possibly stop him from pulling me?"

Andrew returned with Buddy and chimed in, "It's not about strength, Emily, it's about tools and technique."

First, George laid out the basic tools of his trade, explaining each. "When a new dog arrives, each one is fitted with a martingale collar. These collars have a loop in them that is very comfortable until they pull. If they pull, it tightens. When they relax, it loosens. If a dog ever tries to run at another dog, the collar will never slip off them, and there's a ring for a normal leash to hook into. This is primarily for safety reasons so that the dogs can never slip out and either hurt another dog, or escape into traffic.

THE LEADERSHIP WALK

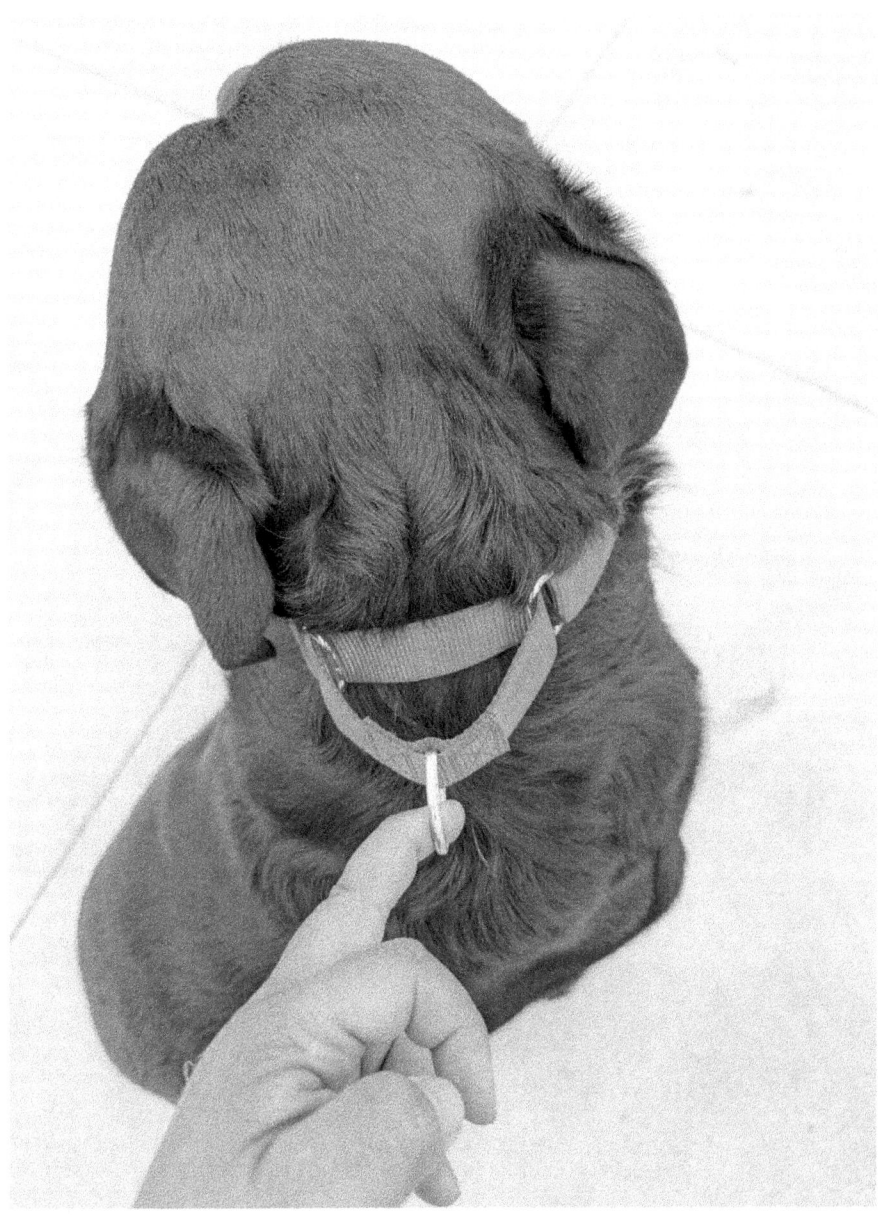

Martingale Collar

"Similarly, we use slip leads for training. Slip leads come in different lengths, and they serve the same purpose as the martingale collars. When a dog is calmly walking by your side, it's loose and comfortable. When they try to lead the walk in a different direction, the lead tightens and discourages the undesirable behaviour.

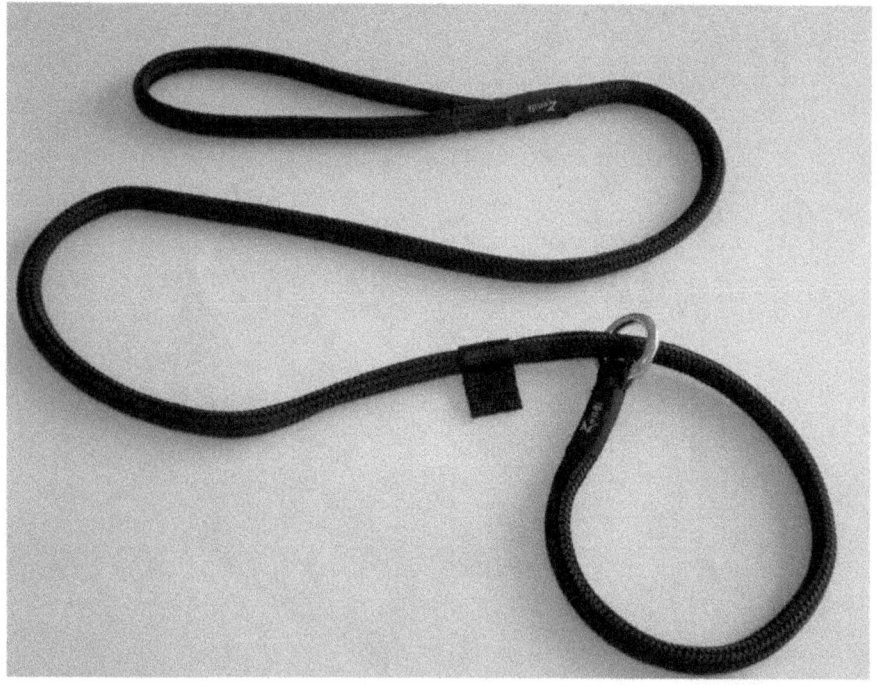

Slip Lead

"Because these tools tightens when the dog pulls, they can't back out of them.

Buckle collars and harnesses leave room for a dog to lunge forward, then reverse back and possibly slip out. Everyone's safety relies upon the proper tools to control and guide the dogs effectively."

George then demonstrated how each was properly put on, adjusted, and used on Buddy. With that, Andrew took Buddy into a levelled training track. As they began to walk, Buddy lunged forward, trying to lead. Andrew, instead of being dragged, shifted into a stance that looked straight out of a martial arts film. He stood sideways, spread his legs shoulder width apart, and lowered his centre of gravity. His balance and poise stopped Buddy's pulling instantly.

The Brace Stance

I watched in awe. Andrew began walking in a different direction. Every time Buddy tried to pull, Andrew assumed that bracing stance and became an immovable force.

As I watched Buddy lunge forward, the slip lead tightening around his neck, a surge of concern welled up inside me. "But won't Buddy hurt himself with the slip lead around his neck like that?" I asked, unable to hide the worry in my voice.

George looked at me with calm assurance and nodded towards Andrew. "Notice what Andrew is doing," he said gently. "He's not pulling back on the leash at all. He's just bracing. All the pressure Buddy feels is self-inflicted. The beauty of this process is that Buddy is in control of the discomfort. He'll soon realise that if he stops pulling, the pressure automatically releases."

I focused on Andrew's movements, paying closer attention this time. It was true—Andrew wasn't yanking or pulling on the leash. He was merely holding his stance, allowing Buddy to determine when the pressure would ease.

George continued, "This teaches Buddy an important lesson: he can undo the discomfort by himself. The moment he stops pulling, the tension on the lead disappears. Andrew isn't using strength to overpower Buddy; he's using technique to guide him. It's all about allowing Buddy to understand that his actions have consequences. The instant he stops pulling, the pressure is gone. Andrew's just holding a stance so that he can withstand Buddy's strength but never pulling back."

I nodded, the logic of it sinking in. "So, Andrew's not causing any pain—he's just letting Buddy figure it out on his own."

"Exactly," George affirmed. "Most people make the mistake of pulling back when their dog pulls. This not only risks injuring the dog but also creates a tug-of-war situation that the dog might see as a challenge. By doing nothing other than stopping and bracing, Andrew is showing Buddy that pulling gets him nowhere and that comfort comes from compliance." It wasn't long before Buddy gave up trying to pull him altogether.

Andrew then introduced a new technique, which he cheekily named, "Where the Heck Do You Think You're Going?" Every time Buddy tried to lead or pull in a particular direction, Andrew braced himself, then guided Buddy to follow him in the opposite direction. It was a mesmerising dance, with Buddy constantly being caught off guard.

The message was clear: Buddy wasn't in charge; Andrew was. I am reminded with what George had said, "a leader leads, and a follower follows."

I was astounded. "I can't believe it," I whispered, my voice filled with awe. "He's like a completely different dog when you're walking him."

Andrew nodded, his eyes still on Buddy. "Most people make the mistake of taking their dogs on a destination walk right away. With the Leadership Walk, we're teaching them the most important lessons first: Respect Leash Pressure. Just follow, don't lead."

He paused, glancing at me. "It's like dancing. In dancing, there's a leader and a follower. The same goes for a Leadership Walk."

"He dances as well?" I mused to myself, suppressing a grin.

As I watched Andrew and Buddy, I realised, "It's not just about walking, is it? With this routine, you're teaching Buddy to follow. You're showing him that he's the follower, not the leader. It's about getting him to submit to the handler's authority."

George smiled with pride. "Exactly!"

In an excited rush of understanding, I enthused, "I see! It's not just about the walk. It's about establishing a relationship based on respect and guidance. And it starts with teaching Buddy to follow."

The profound simplicity of the routine hit me. This wasn't walking a dog; it was about building a bond based on mutual respect. It is about leading and guiding Buddy and not having Buddy lead me.

George decided to delve deeper into the Leadership Walk concept. "Emily, before you even think about taking Buddy out on the streets, you need to master the Leadership Walk in a controlled environment. You've seen Andrew's 'Where the Heck Do You Think You're Going?' routine. That's just one part of it. The brace and change direction routine is crucial. It's all about teaching Buddy that you're in charge, that he needs to follow your lead."

You can learn more about how to do a Leadership Walk and more advanced techniques, including George's 7-point method, with step by step instructional videos at www.DogLeadershipAcademy.com

We also have a specific step by step video series that teaches you how to force free loose leash walk your dog at DogLeadershipAcademy.com.

Simply "Sign Up" to get started.

"So," I summarised, "This isn't about going somewhere, it's about establishing leadership in a gentle, non-confrontational manner. Before we can actually walk somewhere, we need to learn HOW to walk."

"Exactly!" George beamed. "Once you feel confident with the Leadership Walk in a controlled space, you can then graduate to your driveway. After that, you can practice in front of your house. The idea is to slowly expose Buddy to more stimuli, ensuring he remains calm and focused on you without getting overstimulated."

I was intrigued. "So, baby steps?"

"Precisely," George affirmed. "Most people make the mistake of letting their dogs lead them everywhere, right on the streets, from day one. They end up being dragged around, reinforcing the dog's belief that they're in charge. Unfortunately, social media has popularised the idea of 'enrichment' and 'sniffari,' where dogs are encouraged to explore and sniff around during walks to get mental stimulation. While this sounds good in theory, it often backfires when dogs haven't first learned to respect leash pressure. Invariably, people end up getting dragged along, sometimes even injuring themselves with muscle strains or worse."

I reflected on the logic of George's method. By taking things step by step, I wouldn't overwhelm Buddy. Instead, I'd be setting us both up for success, helping him—and me—maintain a calm demeanour throughout the process.

It was a revelation. Here was a method that seemed so simple, yet so effective. It was about building a bond of trust and respect, ensuring that Buddy viewed the handler as the leader.

"Thank you," I whispered, emotionally. I looked George straight in the eyes, "I'm ready to start this journey with Buddy."

George smiled, placing a reassuring hand on my shoulder. "You've got this,

THE LEADERSHIP WALK

Emily. Just remember, it's all about patience, consistency, and love."

"I'm in! What do I do first? What are the rules of a Leadership Walk?"

George began outlining the rules of the Leadership Walk. "First and foremost, let Buddy do his business. He'll concentrate better once that's out of the way. When the Leadership Walk begins, from that moment on, you're both working. Think of it as Buddy being 'on duty.' **This means no sniffing, no peeing, no pulling, and no stopping**. You set the pace, not Buddy dog.

I raised an eyebrow, "Isn't that a bit, I don't know, cruel? What about his enrichment? Dogs need to sniff and explore their environment, right?"

George smiled, a knowing look in his eyes. "That's a common response. People often emphasise enrichment, which is indeed important. Here's the thing: enrichment shouldn't come at the expense of a dog disregarding or disrespecting their handler. It's about balancing rights and responsibility. Too often, people talk about rights, yet they don't talk about the responsibility that goes with those rights. A Leadership Walk teaches the dog to have the responsibility of being respectful so they earn the right to sniff and roam around once the work is done."

He paused, allowing the words to sink in before continuing, "After the Leadership Walk, which typically lasts **about 15 minutes or so**, you can dismiss Buddy. If he behaved well during the walk, reward him by allowing him some free time to sniff and explore. Even then, he's not allowed to drag you around.

"It's all about balance," George added, reading my thoughts. "We're not trying to suppress Buddy's natural behaviours. We're teaching him when it's appropriate to engage in them. Think of the Leadership Walk as a form of mental, as well as physical, exercise. It challenges him to focus, to pay attention to you, and to resist his impulses. Once he's proven he can do that, he gets the reward of free time."

I nodded, appreciating the logic behind the approach. "It makes sense," I admitted. "It's like teaching a child discipline and boundaries. Once they've shown they can behave, they get some playtime."

"Exactly," George affirmed. "And just like with children, consistency is key.

The more consistent you are with the rules, the quicker Buddy will learn and the stronger your bond will become."

With a renewed sense of purpose, I looked at Buddy, who was watching us attentively. "Alright," I said with determination, "let's get to work."

Chapter Summary

This chapter delves deep into the psychology of dogs and the importance of establishing a clear leadership role when walking them.

Key Concepts:

1. **Learned Behaviour**: Dogs, like humans, adopt behaviours that have been successful for them in the past. For instance, if a dog learns that pulling leads its handler forward, it will continue to pull.
2. **Success Strategy**: This term refers to behaviours that are reinforced because they produce a desired outcome. Just as a child might cry to get candy, a dog might pull or bark to get what it wants.
3. **Retraining Belief Systems**: The goal is to teach the dog that old behaviours, like pulling, no longer yield the desired results. This is done through consistent correction and redirection.
4. **Technique Over Strength**: Andrew demonstrates that stopping a dog from pulling isn't about physical strength but rather about the bracing technique. By positioning oneself correctly and using balance, even a strong dog can be prevented from pulling.
5. **Walking Equipment**: George advises against using harnesses for walking dogs, citing their origin in sled-pulling and the potential for dogs to pull owners without consequences. He also points out the safety concerns with harnesses, as dogs can easily slip out of them.
6. **Recommended Collars**: Regular collars are suitable, but slip leads or martingale collars are preferable as they prevent dogs from breaking

free. Retractable leashes are discouraged due to safety concerns, and leashes with elastic components are not recommended as they can hinder communication between the dog and handler.
7. **Leadership Walk**: This is <u>the quickest and easiest way</u> to establish leadership and respect from your dog. This is a controlled walk where the dog is taught to follow the handler's lead. It's likened to a dance, where there's a clear leader and follower. The dog learns not to pull, sniff, or stop unless allowed by the handler.
8. **Learn the Fundamentals**: <u>DO NOT HAVE A DESTINATION!</u> Before taking your dog for a walk with a destination, it is important to teach them the fundamentals of walking first. They need to learn to follow and respect leash pressure first. This means teaching them that they should stop when they get to the end of the leash, not pull harder.
9. **Gradual Exposure**: Before exposing a dog to various stimuli on the streets, it's essential to master the Leadership Walk in a controlled environment. This ensures the dog remains calm and focused on the handler. Gradually increase the stimuli at the pace that your dog can handle with the **goal of setting them up for success at all times**.
10. **Balancing Rights and Responsibility**: While dogs have a natural instinct to explore and sniff, it's crucial to balance this with the responsibility of being respectful to the handler first. After a successful Leadership Walk, dogs can be rewarded with free time to explore.
11. **Consistency is Key**: Just as with training children, it's vital to be consistent with dogs. The more consistent the handler is with the rules of the Leadership Walk, the quicker the dog will learn and adapt.

Rules of the Leadership Walk

1. Business First: Before the Leadership Walk begins, allow the dog to do its business.
2. On Duty: Once the Leadership Walk starts, the dog is considered "on duty." This means the dog is working and should be focused.

3. No Distractions: During the Leadership Walk, the dog should not engage in sniffing, peeing, pulling, or stopping. To minimize distractions, you should start and master the walk in your yard first. **DO NOT GO ANYWHERE UNTIL YOUR DOG HAS LEARN TO RESPECT LEASH PRESSURE.**
4. Setting the pace: You set the pace, not your dog. Be mindful not to speed up to keep up with your dog. If you find that your dog is in front of you, stop and turn around.
5. Balance of Rights and Responsibility: While dogs have the right to enrichment like sniffing and exploring, they also have the responsibility to respect their handler. The Leadership Walk emphasises this balance, teaching dogs to earn their rights by fulfilling their responsibilities.
6. 15-20 minutes: After 15-20 minutes, you can dismiss your dog and allow them free time to sniff and be a dog, but only if they haven't pulled or dragged you around. If they do, get them back into the Leadership Walk.

The chapter emphasises the importance of mutual respect and trust in the handler-dog relationship. Through the Leadership Walk, handlers can establish clear boundaries and leadership, ensuring a harmonious bond with their canine companions.

For more step by step videos on how to do a Leadership Walk, come to www.DogLeadershipAcademy.com.

For more resources, guides, videos and personal coaching come to
www.DogLeadershipAcademy.com

Use Phone to Scan QRCode

9

Comfort vs. Correction

We had worked all morning on our Leadership Walk skills. The sun was high in the sky as we enjoyed a shady break. Birds serenely chirped from the trees, and a gentle breeze cooled us while we sipped water and talked about the different training leads and collars we would be using.

One of George's staff emerged from behind the building, a sleek black Labrador trotted obediently by her side. The moment Buddy caught sight of the newcomer, his entire demeanour changed, the tranquillity suddenly shattered. His muscles tensed, his ears perked, and low growl rumbled in his throat, escalating quickly into a series of sharp barks. Before I could react, Buddy lunged forward, straining against his leash, his eyes locked onto the Labrador.

Panicking, I tried to soothe him. "Buddy, it's okay," I murmured as I dug my heels in trying to maintain my brace as Andrew had shown me.

In a flash, Andrew was by my side. He swiftly took Buddy's leash from my hands and began leading him away on a Leadership Walk. I stood there, stunned, watching as Andrew expertly redirected Buddy's focus, guiding him away from the other dog and back into the Leadership Walk routine.

Seeing my confusion, George approached me, his expression understanding. "You made a common mistake," he began gently. "One that many dog owners make."

I looked at him, waiting for an explanation.

"When Buddy reacted to the other dog, you tried to comfort him," George continued. "But in doing so, you inadvertently reinforced his inappropriate behaviour. Instead of guiding him on how to behave, you essentially told him that his reaction was okay."

I blinked, processing his words. "But I was just trying to calm him down," I protested.

George nodded. "I understand. It's a natural instinct to want to comfort. In situations like this, it's crucial to provide guidance and correction, not comfort. By comforting Buddy, you unintentionally communicated that his aggressive behaviour was acceptable."

I felt a pang of guilt. "I didn't realise," I admitted.

George smiled reassuringly. "It's a learning process, for both you and Buddy. The key is to recognize these moments and learn from them. Remember, dogs don't understand our words in the same way we do, they interpret our actions and energy. In that moment, Buddy needed guidance and leadership, not comfort."

I watched as Andrew continued working with Buddy, redirecting his focus and energy. The Labrador was long gone, yet the lesson remained. I took a deep breath, determined to learn from my mistake and provide Buddy with the guidance he needed.

George took a moment, searching for the right words. "Let me give you an analogy," he began, his gaze thoughtful. "Imagine you're teaching a child to ride a bike. The child tries to ride without holding the handlebars, which is dangerous. Each time they do it and wobble, instead of correcting them, you tell them it's okay and they are doing great. What do you think the child learns?"

"They'd think it's okay to ride without holding the handlebars," I replied.

"Exactly," George affirmed. "By comforting them in that moment, you're unintentionally reinforcing the dangerous behaviour. The child doesn't understand the potential consequences; they just know that when they let go of the handlebars, they get comforted. So, they continue to do it.

"Similarly, when Buddy reacted aggressively to the other dog, and you comforted him, in his mind, he associated his aggressive behaviour with comfort and your approval. He didn't understand that his behaviour was inappropriate; he just knew that when he barked and lunged, he received affection and support."

I nodded. "So, by comforting him, I was essentially telling him that his behaviour was okay."

George smiled gently. "In a way, yes. It's not that you can't comfort Buddy, but it's essential to choose the right moments. When he's displaying inappropriate behaviour, that's the time for guidance and redirection, not comfort. It's about helping him understand what's expected of him and guiding him toward the right behaviour in a timely manner without panicking."

The analogy made it clear. I had unintentionally been reinforcing Buddy's negative behaviour. It was a hard pill to swallow, though I was grateful for George's insight. I was determined to learn and ensure Buddy received the right guidance moving forward.

George noticed the puzzled look on my face as I watched Andrew briskly walk Buddy around the field. "You're wondering why Andrew immediately took Buddy on a Leadership Walk, aren't you?" he asked.

I nodded, "Yes, it seemed so sudden."

George leaned in slightly, his voice calm and explanatory. "When Buddy reacted to the other dog, he was in a heightened state of arousal and aggression. In that state, he wasn't thinking clearly or rationally. The Leadership Walk is a tool we use to snap a dog out of that mindset and bring them back to a focused, working mental state."

He continued, "By taking Buddy on a Leadership Walk, Andrew was essentially telling him, 'You're on the job now Buddy. Focus on me and nothing else.' It's a way to redirect Buddy's attention from the other dog and back to the task at hand. The Leadership Walk demands Buddy's full attention, making him concentrate on keeping pace with Andrew and following his lead."

"So, the Leadership Walk is like a reset button?" I asked.

George smiled, "Exactly. It's a way to reset Buddy and bring him back to a calm, focused state. When a dog is in 'work mode,' they're less likely to

COMFORT VS. CORRECTION

be distracted by external stimuli, whether it's another dog, a cat, or a loud noise. The Leadership Walk reinforces the idea that when they're on the leash, they're working, and their primary focus should be on their handler."

I watched as Buddy, under Andrew's guidance, began to calm down, his attention solely on Andrew and the walk. The transformation was remarkable. "It's amazing how quickly he calms down with the Leadership Walk," I remarked.

George nodded, "It's a powerful tool. And with practice, you'll be able to use it effectively with Buddy whenever he gets distracted or agitated. It doesn't require a lot of space, either. You can Leadership Walk in a hallway, or even in your living room. Remember, it's all about guiding him, focusing him, and showing him the right way to behave and getting him to follow, not lead.

"You see, Emily, dogs, much like people and children, seek guidance in situations they find challenging or unfamiliar. When they're unsure or anxious, they look to their handlers and leaders for direction. It's in their nature."

He paused for a moment before continuing, "When Buddy saw that other dog and reacted, he was essentially facing a crisis in his mind. In such moments, dogs need clear instructions, not comfort. They need to know what's expected of them and be told what to do."

"So, when Andrew took Buddy and started the Leadership Walk, he was essentially giving Buddy the guidance he needed." I concluded.

"Exactly," George affirmed. "Andrew stepped in as the leader, showing Buddy how he should behave in that situation. The Leadership Walk was his way of communicating to Buddy, 'This is what I want you to do right now.' It's a clear, direct instruction that Buddy can understand and follow."

George took a deep breath, "You know, Emily," his voice tinged with a hint of sadness, "most of the dogs I work with, especially those who present with behavioural problems, are simply misguided. They've been through situations where they needed leadership, and they didn't get it."

He looked directly into my eyes, emphasising the gravity of his words. "In crisis situations, when they're anxious, scared, or reactive, they look to their handlers for direction. And when they don't receive that guidance, they try to handle things in their own way which often leads to undesirable behaviours."

I nodded, thinking of Buddy's reaction earlier and my own misguided attempt to comfort him.

George continued, "By stepping in and providing that guidance, especially when they need it most, you're not just addressing the immediate situation. You're building a foundation of trust, respect, and leadership. The dog learns that, in moments of uncertainty, they can look to you for direction. And when they realise they can depend on you to lead them, you earn their respect."

He paused, letting the weight of his words sink in. "Being a leader for your dog isn't about dominance or control. It's about understanding, communication, and guidance. It's about being there for them when they need you most and showing them what to do."

I took a moment to absorb everything George had shared. It was a profound realisation, understanding the depth of the relationship between a dog and their handler. It wasn't just about training commands or having someone to cuddle on the sofa; it was about building a bond based on mutual respect and trust.

I hesitated for a moment, collecting my thoughts. "You know, George," I began, "I watched a lot of 'treat based' dog training videos before meeting you and Andrew. They had a completely different approach."

George raised an eyebrow, inviting me to continue.

"One of the techniques I came across was to scatter treats on the ground when a dog sees another dog. The idea was to distract the dog and redirect their attention."

George nodded, indicating he was familiar with the method.

I continued, "While I understand the concept of redirection, it felt… superficial. It was all about the treat, the distraction. There was no mention of leadership, guidance, or addressing the root cause of the dog's reaction. It was like putting a band-aid on a wound without cleaning it first."

George leaned back, taking in my words. "That's a common approach in many videos and treat based training methods. The idea is to create a positive association with the stimulus, in this case, another dog. By scattering treats, they hope to make the dog associate the sight of another dog with something positive; much like the techniques we discussed earlier in Marker Training and classical conditioning methods."

I frowned, "But that doesn't address the underlying issue, does it? If a dog, like Buddy, were to react aggressively or fearfully towards another dog, simply distracting him with treats doesn't teach him how to behave appropriately in that situation."

"Exactly," George replied. "While treats can be a useful tool in training, they shouldn't be the only tool. Dogs need guidance, especially in challenging situations. Besides, when a dog is in a heightened state, they often are not interested in treats. Whereas with good leadership, we can snap them out of it and teach them how to get out of their mental crisis. By simply distracting them, we're not teaching them how to cope or behave. We're just avoiding the issue. There is no reason we can't use both. We can offer them guidance and then reward them with treats and praise for being calm and not paying attention to the other dog once we get your dog out of the situation."

I thought back to the videos I'd watched, realising their limitations. "It's like they're suggesting we bribe them for temporary good behaviour rather than teaching them what to do and how to overcome the stressor."

George nodded in agreement. "Leadership and guidance are essential. Dogs look to us for direction. If we only rely on distractions, we're missing an opportunity to truly connect with our dogs and guide them through challenges."

I took a deep breath. My mind began to connect the dots, and I found myself reflecting back on the Leadership Walk that Andrew had demonstrated. The Leadership Walk wasn't just about walking; it was a foundational exercise that set the tone for the entire relationship between the dog and the handler.

"It all ties back to leadership and respect," I concluded. "The Leadership Walk is the foundation. It's the starting point from which everything else flows. If we can get that right, everything else becomes so much easier."

George's eyes twinkled with pride. "You've got it, Emily. It's a journey, and every step you take on that Leadership Walk is a step toward building a stronger, more trusting relationship with Buddy."

The sun hung low as I drove Buddy back home, the golden hues illuminating the sky with a warm glow. The day had been filled with revelations, and my mind was buzzing with all the information George and Andrew had shared. As I pulled into my driveway, I felt a mix of excitement and nervousness. I was eager to put into practice what I had learned outside the security of George's training facility, yet anxious about how Buddy would respond.

I unlocked the back gate and led Buddy directly into the yard. With a deep, centering breath, I reminded myself of the techniques George and Andrew had demonstrated. I slipped the lead over Buddy's head, ensuring it sat high on his neck, just behind his ears. With a firm grip on the leash, I began our Leadership Walk.

I started with the bracing technique, then I took a few steps forward. As expected, Buddy tried to pull ahead, but I quickly shifted my weight, grounding myself in the stance Andrew had shown me. To my astonishment, Buddy stopped in his tracks, looking up at me with a puzzled expression as if he is asking me for instructions on what to do next, the technique had worked!

Feeling more confident, I decided to try the 'where the heck do you think you are going?' method. Each time Buddy tried to lead or pull in a particular direction, I braced myself and then turned in the opposite direction. The first few times, Buddy seemed taken aback, but he quickly caught on and fell into step with me. Instead of trying to lead, he began to watch me closely, waiting for cues and following my lead.

As we continued our walk around the yard, I marvelled at the transformation. Buddy, who had dragged me all over the place just two days ago, was now walking calmly by my side, attentive and responsive. The techniques not only worked, they were incredibly effective.

The sun had fully set by the time we finished our practice session. As I removed Buddy's slip lead, I felt a surge of pride. Today had been a turning point in both Buddy's training and in our relationship. The Leadership Walk had laid the foundation for a bond based on mutual respect and trust. I looked down at Buddy, his tail wagged and eyes shone with affection, I knew we were on the right path.

For a more detailed guide and video instructions on how to force free and loose leash walk your dog, come to www.DogLeadershipAcademy.com.

Chapter Summary

In this chapter, the setting is a serene training field where Emily encounters a challenging situation with her dog, Buddy. When Buddy reacts aggressively to another dog, Emily's instinct is to comfort him, however, she learns a valuable lesson about the importance of guidance and leadership in dog training.

1. **Stop Reinforcing Negative Behaviour**: When Buddy reacts aggressively to another dog, Emily's instinct is to comfort him. George explains that by doing so, she inadvertently reinforces Buddy's negative behaviour, making him think his reaction was acceptable.
2. **The Power of Guidance**: In moments of uncertainty or aggression, dogs seek and need guidance. Instead of comforting them, it's crucial to provide clear instructions and leadership. This helps the dog understand the expected behaviour in challenging situations.
3. **Leadership Walk as a Reset**: When Buddy becomes aggressive, Andrew immediately takes him on a Leadership Walk. This serves as a reset button, redirecting Buddy's focus and bringing him back to a calm state. The Leadership Walk demands the dog's full attention, reinforcing the handler's leadership role.
4. **The Limitations of Distraction**: Emily recalls the treat based dog training videos that advocate for using treats as a distraction. While treats can be useful, relying solely on them doesn't address the root cause of a dog's reaction. George emphasises the importance of using both guidance and rewards.
5. **Leadership and Respect**: The chapter underscores the significance of leadership in dog training. Dogs, like children and humans, seek guidance in unfamiliar or stressful situations. By providing clear direction, handlers can build a bond based on mutual respect and trust.

Get Your Free Companion Workbook!

Download the *Beyond Treats Companion Workbook* for practical, step-by-step exercises, daily training guides, and self-assessment tools to help you transform your relationship with your dog. Visit www.dogleadershipacademy.com to get your free copy today!

10

Levelling Up, Drills and Staging Events for Training

The familiar chords of Don't Stop Believin' filled the room, rousing me from my slumber. The first rays of dawn peeked through the curtains, casting a soft peachy glow. As I reached out to silence the alarm, a thought crossed my mind – why had I been so eager to change this tune? This song, with its message of hope and perseverance, had become a beacon for me, my inspiration.

The journey I had embarked upon, following my passion, felt like a dream. While I wasn't in the most comfortable financial position, the savings and the holiday pay from my previous job were my lifeline. They provided me with the freedom to chase my dream without the immediate pressure of income, along with a number of significant nips and tucks to my expenses to make the money stretch.

I sat up, reflecting on the past two weeks. The challenges with Buddy, the lessons with George and Andrew, and the incredible transformation we had both undergone. All of it seemed to resonate with the lyrics of the song. The struggles, the belief in a better tomorrow – it all mirrored my own experience. Even the name of the band, Journey, reflected the journey both Buddy and I shared. It was perfect.

How could I even think to change the song? It seemed like a rejection of the message I so clearly needed, heeded, and seeded. I had zero intention to stop believing. Especially when belief and hope had played such pivotal roles in turning our lives around.

I swung my legs over the side of the bed and bounced to my feet with a renewed sense of purpose. The song wasn't just a catchy tune; it was my daily reminder. A reminder to keep believing, to keep pushing forward, no matter the odds. It symbolised the journey Buddy and I were on, the progress we had made, and our continued breakthroughs.

As I went about my morning routine, the song's chorus played in my mind. The words to Don't Stop Believin' echoed as Buddy and I carried on with our morning routine. Bathroom, breakfast, and a backyard Leadership Walk, for starters. I began to sing aloud, the beat of the song set the pace of our walk. Buddy seemed to pick up on my upbeat mood, his steps more confident, more relaxed, fell easily into cadence with me.

My confidence bolstered, I decided to take our training a step further. With Buddy by my side, we ventured to the front of the house. The familiar surroundings of our yard gave way to the wider world, and I could sense Buddy's heightened awareness. The sights, sounds, and smells of the neighbourhood were all new stimuli for him.

Initially, our Leadership Walk at the front went relatively well. We had a few hiccups, a couple of moments where Buddy's attention wavered, but with some guidance and correction, we managed to get back on track. His progress boosted my confidence, and I thought, "Why not push the boundaries a bit further?"

I decided to take Buddy for a walk around the block. The first few metres were manageable but, as we ventured further from the familiar territory of our home, Buddy's demeanour began to change. The lead grew taut as he pulled ahead, ears perked up, and tail wagging with excitement. The calm, composed dog I had been walking moments ago was slowly replaced by an excitable, overstimulated version.

I tried to recall the techniques George and Andrew had taught me. I braced myself, attempting the 'Where the Heck Do You Think You're Going' method, yet Buddy's excitement seemed to override his training. Each passing car, chirping bird, and distant bark seemed to draw his attention, making it increasingly difficult for me to regain control.

My heart raced as I felt the situation escalating. The more I tried to correct Buddy, the more agitated he became, and the more frustrated I became. It was clear that I had overestimated our progress and had put us in a situation that neither of us was prepared for.

I regrettably realised my mistake – I had pushed Buddy past his threshold. I should have taken things slower, ensuring Buddy was fully comfortable and responsive in one environment before introducing him to a more challenging one. In my eagerness to see progress, I had pushed too far, too fast.

I took a deep breath and decided to cut our walk short. Gently yet firmly, I turned Buddy around and we began the slow walk back home. Every step was a struggle, and we needed to loop around in a crazy dance of 'Where the Heck Do You Think You're Going?' to reign in the looming battle of wills. Eventually, we made it back to the safety of our yard.

As I removed Buddy's lead, I took a moment to reflect. This experience was a stark reminder that training was a journey, not a destination. There would be setbacks along the way yet, with patience, consistency, and belief, we would get there. Today was just one of those days, a small bump in our long road ahead.

We both had nice, cooling drinks of water, then settled into remaining sofa cushions together. As I scritched behind Buddy's soft ears, I tried to make sense of Buddy's behaviour. As an avid video gamer and a ranked Fortnite player, I was well-acquainted with the concept of levelling-up. In games, a new character is restricted to entry level areas. If they wandered into a more challenging area, their character would struggle, they'd soon be outmatched and overwhelmed.

The team Buddy and I made together were still entry level characters. Buddy may have had an unknown number of unhealthy, stressful previous experiences in his life before I met him. Even though he had recognised me as his leader, all those past stressors challenged his ability to relax out in public. We were slowly gaining confidence together, pushing past his previous thresholds. Today, I had mistakenly pushed him into a higher-level environment before he was ready, and the stressful result was a clear indicator.

I remembered the first time I joined a gym. I had grabbed the heaviest weights I could manage and I'd overdone it – the next day, I could barely move. It took me a few days to repair the damage I'd done to myself. I realised that, without the proper foundation, I had no business pushing it to the point of hurting myself. I returned and took it much slower, allowing myself to level up to the heavier weights and greater endurance.

In the same vein, Buddy was a beginner and I'd thrown him into an advanced setting too soon. The world outside was a whirlwind of stimuli and challenges he wasn't prepared for. Just as I wouldn't take a Level 1 character into a high level zone in Fortnite, nor slap the heaviest weights into the hands of a gym newbie, Buddy needed a gradual introduction to more challenging environments. He needed to master one level before moving to the next.

This realisation was a game-changer for me. Training Buddy wasn't just about teaching commands; it was about understanding his thresholds and ensuring he was ready for each new challenge. It was a journey, and like any journey, each step mattered. I needed to ensure we took them in the right order, building a strong foundation for the challenges ahead.

I recalled our initial crate training sessions. At first, Buddy was apprehensive about the crate. Instead of forcing him into it, we started with short, positive experiences. He'd spend a few minutes inside with a favourite toy or treat, gradually increasing the time as he became more comfortable. It was all about ensuring he was below his stress threshold, making each experience a positive one. Buddy had levelled up to truly enjoying and feeling safe and happy in his crate.

Similarly, with his barking, I remembered the initial stages. Instead of scolding him every time he barked, I began by identifying what triggered his barking. Then, I'd expose him to that trigger at a distance or lower volume, something where he noticed it, yet didn't react. Over time, as he became desensitised, I gradually increased the intensity, always ensuring it was below his stress threshold.

It all made sense. Buddy needed gradual exposure and training so he accumulated the proper skills to handle various new or potentially stressful situations. Pushing him too fast would only set him up for failure. By levelling him up, step by step, ensuring he was comfortable and confident at each stage, I was setting him up for success.

That afternoon, I guided Buddy into the street several times for short Leadership Walks. With encouragement and limited engagements, I sensed his nervousness recede. We'd worked hard, and I'd tired Buddy out quite a bit, yet we had another big event before the night was through.

As the setting sun painted the sky with hues of orange and pink, I had Buddy on his slip lead, ready for Sally's arrival. I had invited her over, eager for her to meet the man in my life. Because of Buddy's past reactions to other dogs, I had suggested Sally leave Benji at home. That was a level of challenge he wasn't ready to meet yet.

When the doorbell rang, Buddy's ears perked up, and he immediately launched into a series of barks and growls. Though my initial instinct was to comfort him, to reassure him that everything was okay, I tamped down that urge. Buddy needed me to be a leader, to guide him through this moment of perceived crisis.

I grabbed Buddy's lead and began a Leadership Walk around the living room to redirect his focus and energy. As we circled the room, I pulled out my phone and called Sally asking her to wait for a few minutes.

Once Buddy seemed a bit more settled, I rang Sally and asked her to knock again. Predictably, Buddy's barking and growling resumed. This time, however, I firmly and calmly told him to knock it off and settle. I didn't shout, I wasn't angry, I simply asserted myself as his leader and his mama.

To my astonishment, Buddy's demeanour changed almost instantly. He looked up at me, his barking ceased, and he sat down, still alert but no longer aggressive. I immediately rewarded him with a YES and lot's of praises. I was so surprised that it worked so quickly.

I walked Buddy, still on his lead, to the front door with me. As Sally stepped inside, her face lit up with excitement at the sight of Buddy. As she eagerly moved forward, arms outstretched, ready to shower him with affection, I noticed something in Buddy's demeanour that gave me pause. His tail was tucked slightly, his ears pinned back, and there was a hint of uncertainty in his eyes. This was too much for him. I quickly stepped between Sally and

Buddy. "Hold on, Sally," I said firmly. "Give him a moment."

Sally looked surprised, yet stopped in her tracks. While Sally seemed confused, I knew I had made the right call. Buddy needed an advocate in that moment, someone to protect him from a situation he wasn't comfortable with. I remembered a vivid, uncomfortable memory from my own childhood. I was at a local fair with mum when an unsavoury looking person approached me. I remember the unease I felt as the person reached out to touch my arm. Before they could make contact, my mum was there, stepping in front of me, her protective instincts in full force. "Back off," she had said with a steely glare. "My daughter is not public property."

That testament to my mother's fierce, protective nature was a foundational memory for me. Now, here I was, protecting and advocating for Buddy. Just because I knew that Sally was no threat to him, she was a stranger to Buddy. Her high-pitched squeals of excitement and quick movement toward him clearly had triggered something from his past.

Sally responded quickly to the delicate situation and stopped in her tracks. "Of course, I understand. I'll give him some space."

I smiled gratefully at her, then knelt beside Buddy, offering him gentle words of reassurance. It was clear to me, now more than ever, that leadership wasn't just about guiding; it was also about protecting and advocating for those in our care. I led Sally into the living room, Buddy on the other side of me. Once he saw I'd allowed this stranger into our space and that I felt comfortable with her, he became calm, yet watchful. I kept the lead on him, just in case. As Sally and I engaged in conversation, Buddy slowly approached her, sniffed her thoroughly, and eventually laid his head on her lap with the expectation of love and pats.

As soon as Buddy indicated he was ready for the attention, Sally didn't disappoint. Before long, Buddy was draped across her lap and Sally had been slathered in kisses. He brought her his favourite toy and they bonded with games of tug and toss. They were smitten with each other by the time Sally left for home.

I reflected upon Buddy's introduction to Sally. It reminded me of my days managing the grocery store where everything was deliberate. We didn't just hope for the best when training new cashiers, we set up mock scenarios. We didn't wait for a real fire to figure out evacuation procedures, we conducted fire drills. Potential situations were anticipated, and appropriate responses were practiced until it became second nature.

Why wasn't I applying the same principle to Buddy's training? **Instead of waiting for real-life situations to test and often overwhelm us, why not set up deliberate training scenarios, much like a stage play or a drill?**

I decided, rather than being caught off guard when guests like Sally arrived, **I would intentionally invite friends over specifically for training sessions**. I could brief them beforehand, let them know that their visit was a training session for Buddy rather than a mere social call. This way, I could rehearse and practice our routine, ensuring that Buddy knew exactly what was expected in such situations. It would be like running a fire drill, but for behavioural training.

I began to plan some of the scenarios I needed to set for Buddy. People acting like delivery folk, Sally arriving with her dog, friends Buddy hadn't met yet acting like tradesfolk entering to make repairs… there were so many situations I needed to train Buddy how to cope with. Buddy needed to level up to deal with random encounters, just like a beginner boxer needed to level up before entering the ring with a heavyweight champion. I couldn't expect Buddy to flawlessly navigate complex scenarios without proper training. Buddy needed me to set up sparring sessions and drills to prepare him. He needed controlled training scenarios where he learned and practiced without the potential dangers of the real deal.

By setting up these behavioural drills, I could control the environment, anticipate potential challenges, and guide Buddy through the desired responses in real time, catching the situation and offering guidance when Buddy needs it most. Over time, these rehearsed behaviours would become ingrained, making real-life situations more manageable. Much like the policies and procedure protocols at the grocery store.

I felt a surge of optimism. With this new approach, I was confident that Buddy and I could navigate any challenge thrown our way. After all, practice makes perfect, and we were about to get a lot of practice.

The next morning, Buddy and I greeted the day with several Leadership Walk training sessions, both in the back yard and out front. Once he was sufficiently tired, I settled him in his crate for the afternoon so I could pay my mum a nice visit. The drive to her house was filled with anticipation, as I was eager to share my recent accomplishments with Buddy and lay out my plan for her first visit to my place. I wanted everything to be super smooth for both of them, so I already had an outline drafted.

I was so excited to share my experiences with Buddy, I didn't initially notice how tired and drawn mum looked. I refilled her teacup and gently asked, "How have you been feeling? Are you all set for your upcoming cruise?"

She sighed, her fingers playing with the edge of her cardigan. "Oh, Emily," she began, her voice tinged with regret, "I've not been feeling my best lately. I've decided to cancel the trip. It's probably just a minor bug, I just don't want to take any chances."

"Mum, you should see a doctor – just to be sure," I pleaded, my voice filled with genuine worry.

She waved off my concern with a dismissive hand. "It's nothing, dear. I'll be fine."

I narrowed my eyes a bit. There was something there, something she wanted to hide. Fine. If she wanted to deflect, I'd allow it for now and ferret it out eventually. I sipped my own tea and resumed my stories about Buddy and all the dogs I was meeting and working with under George and Andrew's tutelage. I had hoped she'd share in my enthusiasm, in the wins Buddy and I had made. As I spoke, however, I noticed the set of her jaw shift to one of overt concern.

"Emily," she interjected, her tone cautious, "I worry about you working with these dogs. They're unpredictable, and some can be quite dangerous. What if one of them bites you?"

I tried to convey the depth of my passion and the sense of purpose this new path offered me, but she cut me off, her voice firm, "You're all excited now, and that's wonderful, but how are you going to turn this hobby into a stable source of income? You really should think about looking for a regular job."

Her words, though she meant well, felt like a splash of icy water. I understood her intentions, her maternal instinct to protect and guide me, yet the doubt in her voice, the lack of faith in my choices, weighed heavily on my heart. The excitement and joy of the visit were washed away. Despite the comfortable, familiar surroundings of my childhood home, I felt unsettled. I had really hoped for mum's approval and enthusiasm. The rest of our visit felt strained, and I left downhearted and concerned.

Chapter Summary

The chapter delves deep into the concept of "Levelling up" in training, emphasising the importance of understanding a dog's thresholds and ensuring they are ready for each new challenge. Emily's interactions with Sally highlight the significance of leadership, protection, and advocacy in dog training.

1. **Resist Pushing Over Threshold**: Emily intended to take Buddy on a walk that was beyond Buddy's threshold, she subsequently struggled, setting both Buddy and Emily back. This highlights the importance of levelling up one step at a time, setting up Buddy for success every step, rather than failure.
2. **Concept of Levelling Up**: Drawing from her gaming experience, Emily realises that Buddy, like game characters, has different levels of training and thresholds. She understands the importance of gradual exposure, ensuring Buddy is comfortable and confident at each stage before introducing him to more challenging environments.
3. **Advocating for your dog**: When Sally visits, Buddy's initial aggressive reaction showcases the importance of leadership and guidance. Emily's decision to step between Sally and Buddy, advocating for his comfort, emphasises the protective role a dog owner must play when in new or stressful situations.
4. **Behavioural Drills**: Reflecting on her past managerial experience,

Emily conceptualises the idea of behavioural drills. Instead of waiting for haphazard real-life situations, she plans to set up controlled training scenarios to rehearse and practice desired behaviours with Buddy. This makes it easier to offer Buddy timely guidance so he knows how to behave in any given scenarios.

Want to Put These Lessons into Practice?

Download the *Beyond Treats Companion Workbook* for step-by-step exercises, daily templates, and self-assessment tools to guide you through Day 1, Day 2, and beyond. Start turning these principles into action—get your **FREE** copy at www.dogleadershipacademy.com!

11

Wax On, Wax Off

As the days progressed, Buddy and I diligently stuck to our routine of Leadership Walks interspersed with planned encounters. Each day was a new lesson, a new challenge, and a new opportunity to strengthen our bond. With every step we took, I could see Buddy's confidence growing, and our connection deepening. We had successfully managed to level up our training, progressing from the confines of my backyard to the bustling streets outside.

One evening, as we ventured a little further from home, I reflected on our journey so far. I chastised myself for my earlier oversight. Buddy had spent most of his life as a backyard dog, shielded from the myriad of sights, sounds, and scents of the outside world yet, in my initial enthusiasm, I had naively tried to introduce him to the overwhelming stimuli of public spaces without proper preparation. How terrifying it must have been for him, being thrust into an environment so alien and chaotic.

Now, with the principle of levelling up guiding our path, I was more attuned to Buddy's needs and limits. Instead of pushing him into situations he wasn't ready for, I learned to read his cues, to understand his thresholds, and to set the pace of our training accordingly. It was no longer about rushing to achieve a goal, it was about ensuring that each step we took was set up towards helping Buddy succeed. As we walked side by side, I felt a surge of pride. We were in this journey together and, with patience and understanding, there was no challenge we couldn't overcome. It also occurred to me that my confidence has grown while guiding and training Buddy. **With each challenge Buddy and I encountered and overcame, we have both become more confident in facing the stimuli thrown at us.**

> *Remember, success builds confidence. Focus on winning little victories in the beginning. This will give both you and your dog more confidence to deal with more and more difficult challenges.*

Every few days, Buddy and I found ourselves at Gracie's Haven, a place that was quickly becoming a second home for us. There, the constant buzz of activity was a testament to the passion that fueled the place.

Our main agenda during these initial lessons was to master the Leadership Walk, how to read the emotions and expressions of the various dogs I trained with, and learn to react appropriately. Under George's watchful eye, Buddy and I strengthened our bond and refined our skills. Andrew was a constant presence, his stoic, professional demeanour, and focused energy contrasted with George's relaxed warmth. Whatever lessons the day held, the most amazing thing about Gracie's Haven was the sense of compassion and love that permeated the air. Every dog, regardless of their behavioural challenges, was treated with kindness and understanding by everyone on site.

All dogs at the facility were clients seeking help, much like patients at a mental health clinic. George and Andrew approached their roles with a seriousness that underscored their commitment to these animals. They viewed each dog's plight with empathy, always striving to provide the best care and guidance. My lessons included the physical practices as well as deep dives into the theory behind dog behaviours, understanding the nuances and intricacies of their actions and reactions.

Though the work was serious and intentional, the atmosphere at the facility was surprisingly informal. Laughter echoed, trainers exchanged playful banter, and there was a genuine warmth that made every visit enjoyable.

Though my days at Gracie's Haven were filled with learning and progress,

WAX ON, WAX OFF

Andrew continued to confuse me. Despite my best efforts to connect with him, he remained distant. It seemed like every encounter he was sizing me up and he found me lacking. I just couldn't make a connection, and that smug, arrogant demeanour of his was beginning to grate on my nerves.

One day, after another session of basic Leadership Walks with the easiest of the dogs at the Haven, I decided to confront him. "Andrew, when do I move on to the more advanced stuff? I feel like I've been doing the same thing over and over."

He looked at me, a hint of amusement in his eyes, and replied condescendingly, "When you're ready, kid. For now, it's 'wax on, wax off' for you."

I blinked. "Wax on, wax off? What's that supposed to mean?"

Andrew chuckled, clearly enjoying my confusion. "It's a reference from The Karate Kid, an Eighties movie. In it, a young boy named Daniel wants to learn karate quickly, but his sensei, Mr. Miyagi, makes him do seemingly mundane tasks like cleaning and waxing cars over and over. He instructs Daniel the arm movement to apply wax on, and the movement to wax off, day after day. Daniel doesn't understand the purpose until later when he realises that these repetitive tasks, these very specific motions he executed, were foundational exercises, teaching him the basic movements, muscle memory and discipline required for self defense."

I considered his reference – It wasn't about rushing through to get to the good stuff, it was about building a strong foundation, one step at a time. And as much as I hated to admit it, Andrew was right. I needed to be patient, trust the process, and focus on mastering the basics before diving into the deep end.

At my thoughtful expression, Andrew continued, "Just like Daniel, you're eager to jump into the exciting stuff. What you don't realise is that the Leadership Walk is the foundation of everything we do here. It's about discipline, leadership, and building trust. By mastering the Leadership Walk with different dogs, you're laying the groundwork for all the advanced training that comes later. It's not just about walking a dog; it's about establishing a relationship based on mutual respect and understanding. Every dog is different, so leading them through the Leadership Walk is a journey.

You think you've been leading the same dog through the same exercise, yet with every walk, both you and the dog change. You are learning to read the dogs, you are learning to adjust to the changes in them and yourself. Have you considered that the exercises seem a bit too easy because you have become more proficient at the practice?"

My jaw hit the ground. Had I? Had I progressed in ways I hadn't been able to measure? I thought about competitive sports, where athletes spent countless hours perfecting their technique, drilling the same movements over and over again until they were second nature. A swimmer, for instance, doesn't just dive into the pool and start racing. They work on their strokes, their turns, their breathing – the foundational elements that, when combined, lead to peak performance.

This emphasis on the basics, on daily practice and consistency, was the key to success. It was a reminder that excellence was never achieved overnight, it was the result of dedication, of showing up every day, and putting in the work, even when it felt repetitive or mundane.

The Leadership Walks with Buddy and the other dogs at the Haven was my 'wax on, wax off' training. It was my foundation, and it was crucial to get these basics right. It wasn't about rushing to the finish line; it was about enjoying the journey, taking it slow and steady, and trusting that with time and consistency, the results would come.

Andrew, with a mischievous glint in his eyes, nodded in George's direction. "He's about to feed Gracie, Max, and Delenn. Why don't you take a moment and watch how he does that."

Curious, I observed through the fence as George brought bowls of food out, set them down on the ground, and without uttering a sound, guided his dogs through exercises. Never once did they approach the food nor break form. With hand gestures alone, George had his dogs shadow him, sit, stay, or wind between his legs. All three focused solely on their leader as instructed them. It was mesmerising. Even as other dogs darted around, playing and barking, Gracie and the Rottweilers remained undistracted, their attention and respect unwavering.

Before releasing them to eat, George had all three stop, sit, and stay. He noticed me at the fence and approached. Despite his back to them, they remained seated, waiting for their next instruction.

I was in awe. "How…?" I began, struggling to find the right words. "How did you train them to be so obedient?"

George chuckled, his eyes twinkling with pride. "Wax on, wax off, Emily," he replied. "Consistency. Every day, we practice the basics. Over and over again. It's not about teaching them a hundred different commands. It's about perfecting the few that matter most." He paused then added, "You know, Bruce Lee once said he wasn't afraid of the person who practiced ten thousand moves. He feared, instead, the man who practiced one move ten thousand times. That's the power of consistency."

The lesson was clear. Mastery wasn't about breadth, it was about depth. It was about honing a skill through relentless practice until it became second nature. And as I watched George's dogs and their unwavering focus, I realised the profound impact of such dedication. George achieved this level of obedience without resorting to treats, without raising his voice, without any form of intimidation. It was pure respect and trust.

I contrasted this with the obedience classes Sally had taken and how unsuccessful their reliance upon treats and ignoring poor behaviour had been for her. The promise of reward is not always a guarantee of obedience and respect.

George's approach was different. The bond he shared with his dogs was immense. It was built on mutual trust, follow through, and consistent training. The dogs didn't obey George because they expected a treat; they obeyed because they respected him as their leader and they saw him as their employer. The fact they sat patiently with their bowls of food a short distance before them was a testament to the trust he had built. They knew that food was theirs, they trusted George and would wait for his release. This was the kind of relationship I aspired to have with Buddy.

After lessons, Buddy and I walked to our car. I removed his leash and buckled him into the back seat. Lost in my own thoughts, I walked around to the driver's side, and drank some water. As I started the car, I noticed that Andrew was heading toward a gleaming red sports car parked a few spaces away from mine. While the car was impressive, the lady waiting behind the wheel was drop dead gorgeous. As Andrew sat in the passenger seat, she beamed a radiant smile at him. He leaned over, kissed her on the cheek, buckled in, and they drove off together.

A sudden, unexpected pang of jealousy surged through me. I blinked in surprise, taken aback by the intensity of the emotion. I chastised myself, reminding myself that I had only met Andrew recently, I had no reason to feel any attachment. If anything, he seemed a bit cold toward me. I cranked up the music and set off for home.

Chapter Summary

In this chapter, Emily's understanding of dog training deepens as she continues her Leadership Walk training.

1. **Leadership Walks** - Emily and Buddy continue their routine of Leadership Walks, emphasising the importance of understanding a dog's comfort levels and pacing the training accordingly. Emily realises the significance of laying a strong foundation before introducing Buddy to more challenging environments.
2. **The "Wax On, Wax Off" Concept** - Andrew introduces Emily to the idea of mastering foundational skills, drawing a parallel to The Karate Kid movie. The Leadership Walk is likened to the repetitive tasks in the movie, emphasising the importance of mastering the basics before progressing.
3. **Gracie, Max, and Delenn's Obedience** - George's relationship with his dogs showcase the pinnacle of obedience achieved through consistent training. Their unwavering focus on George, without the lure of treats, highlights the deep bond formed through mutual respect and trust.
4. **True Obedience vs. Bribery** - Emily reflects on the difference between genuine obedience based on respect vs. obedience achieved through

treats. George's relationship with his dogs, built on trust and consistent training, serves as an aspirational model for Emily's journey with Buddy. Treat based models are more mercenary and transactional in which a dog only performs if it expects to be paid.

Want to Deep Dive Into the Secrets and Principles of Dog Leadership?

For a more detailed exploration of the concepts covered in this chapter, download your **FREE** copy of the **Dog Leadership Training Guide** at www.dogleadershipacademy.com.

This guide reveals:

- **The Secrets of Leadership:** Gain a deeper understanding of how to earn your dog's respect and trust.
- **In-Depth Principles:** Explore the science and philosophy behind leadership-based training.
- **Actionable Strategies:** Step-by-step instructions to address problem behaviors and build a stronger bond.

Don't miss this opportunity to deepen your knowledge and enhance your training. **Visit** www.dogleadershipacademy.com **today to download your free copy!**

12

Jumping on Guests

I wanted the relationship between Sally and Buddy to be strong, so I set up a few arranged dates for Sally to help me practice front door etiquette. One evening, as the sun began to set, there was a familiar knock on the door. Buddy's ears perked up instantly, and I could see the recognition in his eyes. He trotted over to the door, tail wagging vigorously, clearly anticipating Sally's entrance.

As I opened the door, Buddy's excitement was evident. I wanted to see how Sally responded, so I didn't instruct him to stay by my side. When Buddy lunged forward to jump up and greet Sally, she quickly turned her back to him. Buddy, thinking it was a new game, continued his attempts to jump and circled around to face her again.

"Why did you turn your back on him?" I asked, calling Buddy to a heel position to give Sally some space.

"That's what they taught us at the obedience school," Sally replied, brushing some of Buddy's fur off her clothes. "They said turning your back would discourage the dog from jumping."

I raised an eyebrow, recalling our previous encounters. "Has that ever actually worked for you?" I inquired, genuinely curious.

Sally hesitated for a moment, then sighed. "No, not really. It clearly didn't stop Buddy, and he's very strong and persistent in his excitement."

The look of distress on Sally's face was unmistakable. When Buddy jumped on her, I could see her discomfort. It wasn't just about a dog being overly enthusiastic, it was about personal boundaries being crossed.

George's words echoed in my mind, "Dogs are predators, Emily. They operate on instinct, and they don't have our sense of morality. They do what feels good to them."

Turning your back on a predator in the animal kingdom is a sign of submission and weakness. And predators, by nature, are drawn to weakness. Dogs would see turning away as an invitation, a sign that she was a victim.

I brought Sally some tea and we settled together in the living room, Buddy comfortably lounging on the floor next to Sally as she scritched his ears, before asking her, "Think about it, Sal, if some creep approached you the way Buddy did, uninvited and invading your space, what would you do?"

Without hesitation, Sally replied, "I'd probably kick him between the legs."

We both laughed, but the point was clear. Sally knew how to stand her ground against humans who posed a threat. "Why not apply the same principle with Buddy, but with your energy, not the intent to harm him?" I suggested to Sally.

The next day, Sally arrived, armed with a newfound confidence. As she entered, her demeanour was different. She stood tall, exuding an assertive energy. When Buddy approached and tried to jump, Sally raised her knee, blocking him. She pushed him away from her and firmly told him no. She used her body language and voice to clearly communicate her boundaries, in essence communicating "This is my space. Back Off!"

After a few attempts, Buddy got the message. He paused, looked at Sally, and then, deciding she wasn't inviting play, he simply walked away. All the previous times Sally had visited, turning her back had never deterred Buddy. Now, with just a change in body language and attitude, without any treats, Sally had communicated her boundaries, and Buddy had respected them.

It was a powerful lesson in the importance of clear communication and assertiveness, not just with dogs, but in all aspects of life.

Sally stood there, astonished. "I can't believe that worked," she murmured, processing the events. "It's just… it's so different from everything I've been taught in obedience school."

BEYOND TREATS: REVOLUTIONARY DOG TRAINING FOR LASTING BEHAVIOUR CHANGE

I saw the gears turning in her head, trying to reconcile the effective method she had just witnessed with the teachings she had received in her classes. "They always told us never to say 'no' or correct a dog for inappropriate behaviour," she mused. "They said it would damage the bond or make the dog fearful."

I couldn't help but smile, recalling our previous encounters and the lessons we'd learned. "Remember the incident with the German Shepherd and Benji at the park? That Shepherd didn't use treats or gentle coaxing. He communicated in a language Benji understood. He set a boundary, and Benji respected it."

Sally nodded, the memory fresh in her mind. "That's just it," she said, her voice rising with passion. "Dogs have their own language, their own way of communicating. It's clear, direct, and effective. Why are these treat based trainers trying to reinvent the wheel with these convoluted training methods? Why are they marketing these confusing messages as being 'backed by science?' it's almost as if they are deliberately making dog training more complicated so clients have to go back to them over and over to so they can make more money.'"

I leaned in, capturing her gaze. "Exactly, Sal. Dogs have been communicating with each other for thousands of years. They have a rich, nuanced language that they understand instinctively. When we step into their world and communicate using their language, we're speaking to them on a level they inherently grasp."

Sally's eyes widened in realisation. "So, all this time, by not correcting Buddy or setting clear boundaries, I was essentially speaking gibberish to him?"

I nodded. "In a way, yes. By using their language, by being clear and assertive, we're not being mean or damaging our bond with them. We're simply being effective communicators. And in the end, isn't that what it's about? Clear communication?"

Sally took a deep breath, "It's just so… logical, I can't believe I never saw it before. You know, Em, I've been attending this obedience class for weeks now, and while Benji does perform the tricks they teach, he only does so when there's a treat involved. It's like I have trained him to be a mercenary. He will only work for treats."

I nodded in understanding, having witnessed similar scenarios with other dog owners. "It sounds like you're experiencing a form of cognitive dissonance," I remarked.

Sally raised an eyebrow, "Cognitive what now?"

"Cognitive dissonance," I repeated. "It's a psychological term that describes the discomfort one feels when holding two contradictory beliefs or attitudes. In this case, you've been led to believe that you are training your dog to be obedient yet, deep down, you recognize that true obedience isn't conditional on treats."

Sally pondered this for a moment. "So, you're saying that because I've been told this is 'obedience training' I've been trying to convince myself that it's true obedience, even though I can see it's not?"

"Exactly," I affirmed. "True obedience comes from a place of respect and understanding between the dog and the handler. It's not about bribing them with treats. It's about building a bond based on mutual trust. When a dog listens to you because they respect and trust you, not because they're waiting for a bribe with treats, that's genuine obedience."

Sally sighed, running a hand through her hair. "It's just so frustrating. I've spent so much time and money on these classes, and now I feel like I've been misled."

I reached over, giving her hand a reassuring squeeze. "It's not your fault, Sal. True training takes time, patience, and understanding. It's about building a relationship, not just teaching tricks."

Sally nodded, taking a deep breath. "Thanks, Em. I think I need to reevaluate my approach to training. Maybe it's time to look for a more holistic method, one that focuses on building that bond you talked about."

I smiled, proud of her for recognizing the need for change. "It's a journey, Sal. And I'm here to support you every step of the way."

Chapter Summary

In this chapter, Emily and Sally delve into the nuances of dog training, particularly the difference between genuine obedience and behaviour motivated by treats. Through Buddy's interactions with Sally, they explore the importance of clear communication, assertiveness, and setting boundaries. The chapter challenges treat based obedience training methods and emphasises the significance of mutual respect and trust in the handler-dog relationship.

1 **Turning the Back Technique** - Sally's method of turning her back to deter Buddy from jumping proves ineffective. Emily highlights that in the animal kingdom, turning one's back can be seen as a sign of submission or weakness.

2 **Assertive Communication** - Drawing parallels to personal experiences, Emily encourages Sally to use assertive body language to set clear boundaries with Buddy. Sally successfully communicates her boundaries, and Buddy respects them without the need for treats or commands.

3 **Questioning Treat Based Training** - Sally expresses frustration with her obedience classes, where Benji's behaviour is treat-motivated. Emily introduces the concept of "cognitive dissonance" and emphasises that true obedience stems from mutual respect and trust, not bribery.

4 **Holistic Approach to Training** - The chapter concludes with Sally's realisation of the need for a more holistic training approach that focuses on building a genuine bond with the dog, rather than just teaching tricks.

For more resources, guides, videos and personal coaching come to
www.DogLeadershipAcademy.com

Use Phone to Scan QRCode

13

Use of Corrections, Timely Guidance and Property Destruction

A few days after our enlightening conversation about obedience and training, my phone buzzed with a call from Sally. Her voice, usually so cheerful and bubbly, was laced with distress. "Emily, I need your help. Benji's annoying the crap out of me."

Without hesitation, I headed over to Sally's place. The moment I stepped through the door, Benji, a whirlwind of energy, lunged at me, trying to jump and smother me with his excited affection. Instead of recoiling or turning my back on him, I stood firm, assertively claiming my space. After a few minutes wherein I communicated to Benji that his behaviour was inappropriate, he finally settled down. Only then did I bend down to greet him, offering gentle strokes and kind words. "You see, Sally," I began, "I rewarded Benji for his calm behaviour, not his excited jumping."

"So, what's been happening?" I asked, following her to the living room.

She sighed deeply, "After the incident at the dog park, I've been too scared to take him back there. And our walks… they've become a nightmare. He pulls so hard he almost chokes himself. It's just so unpleasant. Now, he's started digging up the yard and chewing on everything in sight."

I listened intently, piecing together the puzzle. "Sally," I began gently, "Benji's destructive behaviour is probably a result of boredom and a lack of exercise. He's got all this pent-up energy and no way to release it."

Sally's eyes widened in realisation. "So, what do I do? How do I fix it so we can walk together without him decapitating himself?"

Recalling my training sessions with George, I shared, "You remember the Leadership Walk technique I told you about? The 'Where the Heck Do You Think You're Going' method? It's not just about teaching a dog to walk without pulling. It's a way to mentally stimulate them, to challenge them, and to drain that excess energy."

Without waiting for a response, I took Benji's leash, latched it to his collar, and began demonstrating in the backyard. With every change in direction, every stop and start, Benji became more attentive, more focused on me. Within fifteen minutes, he was walking by my side, his leash slack, his attention unwavering.

Sally watched in awe. "I can't believe it," she whispered.

I smiled, handing the leash back to her. "A Leadership Walk does wonders, Sally. It not only teaches them to walk properly, it also mentally exhausts them. Benji's destructive behaviour is a cry for help. He's bored and under-exercised. With regular Leadership Walks, even just in your backyard or driveway, you'll see a change."

To get a complete step by step guide and instructional video of doing a leadership walk correctly, come to www.dogleadershipacademy.com.

Returning to Sally's couch, I took a deep breath, preparing to delve into the intricacies of dog behaviour. "Sally, first and foremost, you need to understand that Benji doesn't know that digging holes or being destructive is bad. In his mind, he's just engaging in natural behaviours. He's completely innocent in this."

Sally looked puzzled. "But he's ruining my garden and my backyard looks like a minefield! Shouldn't he know better? I have scolded him."

I nodded, "I understand your frustration, but think about it this way: dogs in the wild don't punish each other for past actions. If we punish Benji for something he did hours ago, he won't connect the punishment with the action. He'll just become fearful of you. Dogs live in the present moment."

I paused, letting that sink in before continuing. "Remember the incident with Benji and the German Shepherd? Dogs correct each other, and it's always timely. The Shepherd didn't wait hours to correct Benji; he did it immediately, in the moment."

Sally frowned, "But how can I correct him if I'm not there in the moment?"

I leaned forward, "Remember when you first came over to meet Buddy? I was unprepared, and the situation was chaotic. Then, in our subsequent meetings, I set up a deliberate scenario, almost like a stage play, to ensure a controlled environment. You can do the same with Benji."

Sally looked sceptical, "How?"

"You need to catch him in the act," I explained. "Monitor him, be vigilant. If you can't supervise him, consider using a crate to prevent further digging and destructive behaviour when you're not around. Let him have backyard time when you're home and watching from a window so, when you do catch him, you can correct him immediately. It's not about punishment, it's about giving Benji timely guidance."

I saw Sally's determination to understand and help Benji, and I wanted to equip her with the best tools possible. "Sally, George taught me a simple yet effective process for behaviour modification. It's called 'Correction, Redirection, and Reward.' Let me break it down for you."

Sally leaned in, her eyes focused intently on me.

"**Correction.** When Benji is engaging in an inappropriate behaviour, like digging, you need to intercept and correct him. This doesn't mean shouting or being angry. It's about timely interruption, like a firm 'No', a clap of your hands or using your leash. The goal is to get his attention and stop the behaviour.

"**Redirection.** Once you've stopped the unwanted behaviour, you need to show Benji what you want him to do instead. This is the redirection part. For instance, if he's digging, after correcting him, you can lead him to a toy or a play activity. It's about channelling that energy into something more

USE OF CORRECTIONS, TIMELY GUIDANCE AND PROPERTY DESTRUCTION

appropriate and positive.

"**Reward.** Now, here's the crucial part. When Benji engages in the desired behaviour, you reward him. I told you about the Marker Training that I had implemented with Buddy. It's a method where you use a specific sound, like a click from a clicker, or a specific word like 'Yes' to mark the exact moment Benji does the right thing. Then, you follow it up with a reward. It could be a treat, praise, or a toy. The idea is to reinforce the positive behaviour."

Sally looked thoughtful. "So, if I catch Benji digging, I correct him with a firm 'No,' then redirect him to his toy, and when he plays with the toy, I mark that moment with a 'Yes' and give him a treat?"

I nodded, "Exactly! It's a process, Sally. And it's important to be consistent. Every time he engages in an unwanted behaviour, you go through the 'Correction, Redirection, Reward' cycle. Over time, Benji will start to understand what behaviours are desired and which ones aren't."

Sally sighed, "It sounds simple, but I guess it requires patience and consistency."

I smiled, placing a reassuring hand on her shoulder. "It does, and every journey starts with a single step. With each step, you're building a stronger bond with Benji and guiding him toward being a well-behaved companion."

Sally smiled, determination evident in her eyes. "Thank you, Emily. I'll definitely work on the 'Correction, Redirection, Reward' cycle. I'm hopeful that with time and consistency, Benji will become the well-behaved companion I've always wanted. Will you show me that Leadership Walk? I want to get started right away!"

I squeezed her hand, "Let's do it! Patience and consistency are key, and I'm here to help."

Chapter Summary

In this chapter, Emily assists Sally in addressing Benji's escalating behavioural issues. Through hands-on demonstrations and in-depth explanations, Emily introduces Sally to effective dog training techniques that emphasise timely corrections, redirection, and rewards. The chapter underscores the importance of understanding canine behaviour, consistent training, and the significance of building a strong bond between the handler and the dog.

Benji's behavioural Issues - Emily identifies the root cause as a combination of boredom and a lack of exercise.

Leadership Walks - Emily demonstrates the power of Leadership Walks in mentally stimulating and exhausting a dog, using Benji as an example. She emphasises that such walks can help in curbing undesirable behaviours.

Understanding Canine behaviour - Emily educates Sally on the importance of timely corrections. She explains that dogs live in the present moment, and punishing them for past actions can lead to confusion and fear.

Correction, Redirection, and Reward:

The most important lesson here is never to punish your dog for after the fact. Always catch your dog and offer corrections to give them timely guidance on what they should and should not be doing. If you can not supervise or catch them in the act, do your best to prevent these from happening while your dog is unsupervised, like putting them in the crate.

1. **Correction**: Timely interruption of the unwanted behaviour, such as a firm 'No' or a hand clap.
2. **Redirection**: Guiding the dog toward a desired behaviour or activity after the correction.
3. **Reward**: Reinforcing the positive behaviour with a marker (e.g., a clicker sound or the word 'Yes') followed by a treat, praise, or toy.
4. **Consistency in Training** - Emily stresses the importance of being consistent in the training process, ensuring that the dog understands which behaviours are desired and which are not.

USE OF CORRECTIONS, TIMELY GUIDANCE AND PROPERTY DESTRUCTION

Want to Deepen Your Understanding of Dog Leadership?

Download the free *Dog Leadership Training Guide* for a comprehensive dive into the principles of leadership-based training. This traditional guide provides clear, actionable steps to help you build trust, respect, and harmony with your dog. Get your free copy today at www.dogleadershipacademy.com!

14

Recall Training

The soft glow of the café lights illuminated the evening as I settled into a cosy corner booth, waiting for Sally. The day at Gracie's Haven had been long and draining, and I was looking forward to catching up with Sally. She arrived shortly, her face lit with her gorgeous smile.

"Emily! Finally, a night out together!" Sally exclaimed, pulling me into a warm embrace.

We caught up for a bit, and then I inquired about Benji, her spirited cavoodle puppy. "How's the training going with him?"

"The training techniques you introduced have been working wonders, especially in our backyard. I have a question about using the long leash to teach Recall. So, you advised we start in the yard with a two metre lead and, if Benji didn't come when I called, I give the leash a bit of a tug to prompt him. I've been using **marker training** as well as paying with **high value treats** like chicken jerky or rotisserie chicken as a treat, he's almost always responsive. While it works great at home, I faced a hiccup at the park recently. I tried to get him to come back, and he just wouldn't. The long leash was out of my reach, and he seemed more interested in everything else around him."

I raised an eyebrow, "**Did you practice the principle of Levelling Up** that we discussed?"

Sally looked down guiltily, "No, I didn't. We had such great success in the backyard that I thought it would be okay to try it at the park."

RECALL TRAINING

I sighed, "Sally, remember what we talked about. Training in a controlled environment like your backyard is very different from an open space like a park with so many distractions. It's like winning a couple school track meets and then thinking you're ready to head for the Olympics. You wouldn't jump straight to a world championship race after a few victories, right?"

Sally chuckled, "You're right, Emily. I got ahead of myself. I'll make sure to practice the Level Up principle and gradually practice recall with Benji in more challenging environments."

```
Want a More Detailed Recall Training Plan?
For step-by-step instructions and a comprehensive action plan to
master recall training, download the Dog Leadership Training
Guide. This free resource dives deeper into the techniques and
strategies you need to ensure your dog reliably comes when called.
Get your copy now at www.dogleadershipacademy.com and take your
training to the next level!
```

I smiled, "I'm glad to hear that, Sally. You're making such great progress with him. Well done."

She took a sip of her coffee, her gaze thoughtful. "How's your training going?"

I hesitated, searching for the right words. "It's great. And, it's also a bit overwhelming. George and Andrew, they're just so knowledgeable. Sometimes I wonder if I'll ever be as good as them. I have moments of doubt, wondering if I'm cut out for this or if I'm just chasing a dream because of my love for Buddy."

Sally reached across the table, taking my hand. "Emily, I would've been lost without you. When I compare what you've taught me in just a few hours to the obedience trainer at that puppy school I attended, you run circles around him. And you're just an apprentice. You already know more about dog training than many certified trainers out there. I wish you could've taught that class."

With a smile that surfaced from the depths of my soul, I squeezed her hand.

"Thank you, Sally. That means a lot."

She grinned, her eyes mischievous. "Now, enough about dogs. What about your love life? I want someone I can double date with."

I blushed, taken aback by the sudden shift. "Well, there's... Andrew. But he is already taken."

Sally's eyebrows shot up. "Oh? Your instructor? Tell me more!"

I laughed, feeling a bit embarrassed. "He's... well, he looks like Thor. You know, Chris Hemsworth? Just not as bulky. He's so reserved, he doesn't talk much and, honestly, a bit of a stubborn jerk at times. Cocky too. I get the feeling that he doesn't like people much. Like he prefers the company of dogs."

Sally piped in, "Yeah, I can see that. People can be jerks and deceptive, there's so much politics, whereas dogs are honest and loyal." She leaned in, a playful smirk on her face. "Besides Em. Admit it. You want a confident man who knows what he wants and takes charge."

I punched her in the arm and we burst into laughter, the worries of the day forgotten as we revelled in the comfort of old friendships and shared memories.

Sally leaned in closer, her eyes dancing with curiosity. "Tell me more," she urged, taking a sip of her drink.

I sighed, playing with the rim of my cup. "Like I said, he's a man of very few words. Always professional. I've never seen him let his guard down at the training centre. He has this really annoying habit of calling me 'kid' all the time. He looks like he is my age. But one evening, when I was just starting out, I saw him outside with another woman. They seemed... close."

Sally raised an eyebrow, her interest piqued. "Oh? Do you think they're together?"

I shrugged, feeling a twinge of jealousy I didn't want to admit. "I'm not sure. He's very private about his personal life, he never talks about anything personal. The way they looked at each other, though, there was definitely a connection."

Sally smirked, teasingly poking my arm. "Sounds like someone's been doing a bit of spying."

I rolled my eyes, laughing. "It's not like that! I just happened to be there. But honestly, Sally, I don't know. There's this... tension between us. Sometimes our eyes meet, and there's this unspoken understanding. But then he'll just turn away and go back to being Mr. Professional."

Sally leaned back, studying me with a thoughtful expression. "You know, Em, sometimes people put up walls to protect themselves. Maybe he's been hurt before, or maybe he's just cautious because of the professional setting. But if there's chemistry, even a hint of it, it's worth exploring."

I bit my lip, contemplating her words. "I don't know, Sal. It's complicated. And I don't want to read too much into things."

Sally smiled gently, reaching out to squeeze my hand. "Just remember, life's too short for 'what ifs.' If you want him, go get him."

Chapter Summary

Recall Training Guide: Combining Positive Reinforcement with Verbal Marker and Follow-Through Techniques

- Recall training ensures your dog comes back to you when called, an essential command for safety.
- Positive Reinforcement with Verbal Marker: Make sure you spend the time to train your dog on the positive marker training as discussed in Chapter 6.
- Start in a quiet environment to minimise distractions.
- Use a clear, consistent command like "Come!" or "Here!"
- As soon as your dog starts moving toward you, mark the behaviour with a verbal marker such as "Yes!" or "Good!"
- Reward your dog immediately upon arrival with high-value treats like jerky or rotisserie chicken.
- Gradually increase distractions as your dog becomes more reliable in responding.
- Follow-Through with a Long Leash: Begin with your dog on a long leash

in an open area.

- Use your recall command. If the dog doesn't respond, use the leash to guide them back to you. Be assertive as necessary. This ensures the dog understands that "Come" isn't optional.

- Over time, with consistent follow-through, your dog will understand the importance of the recall command.

- Using High-Value Treats: High-value treats like jerky or rotisserie chicken are more enticing than regular treats. Using these makes coming back to you more rewarding for the dog, reinforcing the desired behaviour.

- Be Enthusiastic: Always sound happy and enthusiastic when calling your dog. Your tone should convey that coming back to you is the best option and a positive experience.

Consistency is Key

- Practice regularly and be consistent in your commands, markers, and rewards.

- Avoid calling your dog for negative experiences, like leaving the park or getting a bath.

- **practice Level Up:** - Start with a low level of distraction first before moving to higher levels of distraction. - Starting at a dog park and expecting your dog to come is a surefire way to fail and you consequently becoming frustrated with your dog. **Don't do it.**

Final Tips:

- Never punish your dog for coming back, even if it took longer than you wanted. Never call your dog while angry, even if you are because you dog was being naughty or disobedient. Always reward your dog for coming.

- Celebrate small successes and be patient. Recall training is a process that requires time and consistency.

15

The Road Trip

The early morning stillness was interrupted by the sudden vibration of my phone. Glancing at the screen, I saw George's name flashing. I quickly answered, and George's voice, tinged with urgency, filled my ears.

"Emily, there's a situation. There is a German Shepard in Canberra, labelled as human aggressive. The pound plans to euthanize him in a few days. I can't leave the facility right now, but I need someone to retrieve him. Can you help accompany Andrew to fetch this dog?"

My heart raced at the significance of the request, but the thought of a dog losing its life due to a label was unbearable. "Umm, sure, I guess."

"Thank you. Meet him at the facility around 7 tomorrow. And don't worry about Buddy; you can leave him with me."

The next day, as dawn painted the sky in shades of orange and pink, I pulled into Gracie's Haven. Andrew was already there, leaning against his SUV, his usual stoic expression in place. The air was thick with tension, yet I was determined to bridge the gap.

"Good morning, Andrew," I greeted pleasantly, trying to infuse some warmth into the situation.

He merely nodded in acknowledgment. "We should head out. Run Buddy down to George and let's hit the road."

The drive was filled with long stretches of silence, punctuated only by the sound of the SUV and the music from Andrew's playlist. I found myself frequently glancing over at Andrew, trying to decipher the thoughts behind his guarded expression.

As the journey continued, the speakers began playing some classic rock tunes. The familiar chords of "Don't Stop Believin'" filled the SUV, and to my astonishment, Andrew began to sing along. He was awful. He was off-key and his timing was abysmal, yet the sheer unexpectedness of the moment made it magical. He dorkily hummed along the parts that he wasn't exactly familiar with, then belted it out, with gusto, the chorus. It was hilarious and adorable.

Unable to resist, I joined in, our voices merging in a spirited duet. For those few minutes, the seriousness of our mission faded, replaced by the shared joy of a beloved song. The two of us, so different in so many ways, found common ground in the melodies of classic rock, reminding us of the power of music to connect and uplift.

Taking advantage of the moment, I hit the repeat button on the console and the song restarted anew. I took the first part, "Just a small town girl, livin' in a lonely world." Looking at Andrew's eyes, I dared him to pick up the tune.

As if on cue, he belted out, "Just a city boy...", and our eyes met. The smile in his eyes made me thankful that I was sitting down lest my legs would have crumbled like an accordion in a cartoon."

As the last notes of the song faded, Andrew and I exchanged a glance, both of us wearing wide grins. The initial tension between us had melted away, and the road ahead suddenly felt less intimidating. Music had bridged the gap, forging a bond that would undoubtedly help us navigate the challenges that lay ahead.

The classic rock playlist continued its roll, setting the tone for our ride south. When "Sweet Caroline" started playing, both Andrew and I couldn't resist singing along, our voices a joyful noise together. The chorus, "Sweet Caroline, ba ba ba," echoed in the vehicle, and our laughter filled the spaces between the notes. Our spirits soared even higher as "Summer Lovin'" from Grease came on, and we belted out the lyrics in duet, lost in the rhythm of the song with me cringing at how terrible and hilarious Andrew was. We both laughed when the song ended.

The mood shifted dramatically as we pulled into the Pound's parking lot. The building exuded a cold, unwelcoming aura, and the distant barking of dogs added to the sombre atmosphere. We approached the front desk, where the staff greeted us with apprehensive looks. They briefed us about Millie, the dog we were there to rescue. The narrative was heartbreaking. Millie had been branded as aggressive merely for barking at a vet behaviourist. This label, coupled with the staff's evident fear, had resulted in Millie being heavily sedated.

Navigating our way to the holding area, the tension was almost suffocating. The staff maintained a wary distance from Millie's enclosure, their expressions a mix of fear and concern. Sensing the need for a calm approach, Andrew signalled for me to stay back. He slowly approached Millie's cell, his every move calculated and non-threatening. He paused to observe Millie, assessing the dog's body language and overall demeanour. It became evident to Andrew that Millie wasn't inherently aggressive; she was just terrified and overwhelmed.

With a display of quiet assurance, Andrew stepped into the cell. He gently placed the slip lead over Millie's head, and together, they exited the enclosure without any drama. The staff watched in stunned silence, their initial expectations of a confrontation shattered by the compassionate understanding they had just witnessed. I beamed with pride at how smoothly Andrew handled it – especially in front of a gobsmacked audience. I handed them a stack of George's business cards and thanked them for giving us a call.

Once outside, Andrew spent some time guiding Millie through a Leadership Walk. Millie's response was heartwarming. She exhibited trust and a willingness to follow Andrew's lead, indicating that with the right guidance, she had the potential to be an incredible companion.

As we secured Millie in the crate in the SUV, a whirlwind of emotions engulfed me. Relief at having rescued Millie was mixed with frustration at the system that had been so quick to misjudge and condemn her. The drive home was a time for introspection and hope, with thoughts centred on giving Millie a fresh start.

The SUV's engine rumbled steadily, occasionally interrupted by our conversation and Millie yawning. As the road stretched out before us, Andrew turned to me, curious.

"So, tell me about yourself, kid. What do you do for fun?" he asked, his tone light and inquisitive.

I hesitated for a moment, wondering how much to reveal. "Well," I began, a playful smirk forming on my lips, "I'm one of those gamer geek girls. I love playing computer games, especially online competitive shooters like Fortnite and PubG."

Andrew's eyebrows shot up in surprise, clearly not expecting that response. "Really? That's... unexpected."

I chuckled, "What did you expect?"

He laughed, "No, no. It's just... you don't strike me as the gaming type."

I raised an eyebrow, "And what exactly is the gaming type?"

Before he could answer, I turned the tables on him. "What about you? What do you do for fun?"

Andrew looked slightly sheepish, "Well, believe it or not, I'm a bit of a gamer myself. I play Fortnite, MMOs, and even D&D. George and I actually play in a campaign together with some other friends."

I blinked in surprise, "Really? George plays D&D? That's... unexpected."

Andrew grinned, "See? We are all full of surprises."

I smirked, "So, are you any good at Fortnite?"

He shrugged nonchalantly, "I'm not bad."

I gave him a condescending look, which he caught immediately. "What?" he asked defensively.

"Oh, nothing," I replied with a sly smile, hinting that I could probably kick his ass in any of those games.

Andrew chuckled, "Challenge accepted."

And just like that, amidst the backdrop of eucalyptus forest and a journey to rescue a dog, two unlikely gamers found common ground.

As the kilometres rolled by, Andrew spoke over Millie's gentle snores, "Kid," he started, a hint of hesitation in his voice, "I've seen many come and go in this line of work. I'll admit, I wasn't sure where you'd fit in." He paused before finally saying, "I think you'll do okay."

I glanced over, trying to gauge the depth of his words. "That's high praise coming from you, Andrew," I replied with genuine appreciation.

A rare smile graced Andrew's usually impassive face. "You've earned it, kid," he affirmed.

His acknowledgment wasn't just a casual compliment. It was a genuine gesture of respect, recognizing the dedication and hard work I had put into my training. For me, it was an affirmation that I was on the right track, that I had discovered my true calling. The path ahead was undoubtedly challenging, but with the support of mentors like Andrew and George, I felt equipped to tackle any obstacle.

After a few moments of silence, I turned to Andrew, "Why do you keep calling me 'kid?' How old are you anyway?"

Andrew looked momentarily taken aback, his eyebrows rising in surprise. "I'm 27," he replied, a hint of defensiveness in his tone.

I couldn't help but laugh. "You're 27? That means you're younger than me! And here you are, calling me kid? Isn't that a bit... arrogant?"

Andrew's face turned a shade redder, and he cleared his throat, searching for the right words. "I... I didn't mean it in a condescending way," he began, looking slightly sheepish. "It's just a habit, I guess."

I smirked, enjoying the slight role reversal. "Well, maybe it's time to break that habit, especially when the 'kid' is older than you."

Andrew chuckled, the tension dissipating. "Point taken. I'll try to remember that."

There wasn't a lot of sunlight left by the time we'd settled Millie at the Haven. I handed George the packet of Millie's medication. He read the instructions and tacked the packet to the bulletin board next to Millie's name and care instructions.

My heart ached as I observed Millie. She fell right back to sleep after a bit of toilet time. "Why is the immediate solution to behavioural issues always medication? It's akin to slapping a band-aid on a gushing wound!"

Andrew exhaled deeply, nodding in agreement. "It's an all-too-common issue, Emily. When confronted with a dog's behavioural challenges, most people instinctively seek out veterinarians. And while vets possess immense knowledge about a dog's physical well-being, they aren't necessarily adept at addressing complex behavioural issues."

I frowned. "But that's like going to a plumber for an electrical problem!"

"That's precisely why George is so passionate about expanding our program," Andrew continued, his voice filled with conviction. "He's working tirelessly to train more behaviourists and even developing an online program to assist dog owners globally."

Andrew continued. "The idea is to provide immediate guidance and support to dog owners around the world, even if they can't access a behaviourist right away. George has dumped all his knowledge, all his processes into the program."

"My friend Sally has been having problems with her Cavoodle puppy. Something like that could really help her. How does it work?"

"It's really simple," Andrew began. "Since it's online, it's always available at any hour of the day, anywhere in the world. This means that you can use it at any time to ask any questions about dog behaviour. It's a query to the program, yet it's as if you are talking directly to George. And the best part is, it's free. This is in line with his mission to help dogs and keep families together. Just tell Sally to go to www.DogLeadershipAcademy.com.

"George envisions a world where well-trained, knowledgeable dog behaviourists are as accessible as local vets. His dream is to have behaviourists in every community, serving to ensure dogs and their humans receive the right kind of help."

I pondered the implications. "That sounds amazing, but wouldn't that lead to more competition among behaviourists?"

Andrew laughed. "Would a vet consider other vets across town as competition? Or do they simply serve their own community?"

I chuckled, too. "No, they just focus on their community."

"Exactly," Andrew replied. "The goal isn't competition. The more behaviourists we have, the more dogs we can save. And in the end, that's what it's all about – ensuring every dog gets a fair chance."

I nodded, deeply moved by the vision. It was clear that this wasn't just a job for Andrew and George; it was a calling. I felt privileged to be a part of this transformative journey.

Chapter Summary

In this chapter, Emily and Andrew discuss the prevalent issue of medicating dogs as a quick fix to behavioural problems because people go to vets for behavioural problems. Every problem can easily be classified as "anxiety." Andrew introduces Emily to George's ambitious plan to make dog behaviourist knowledge more accessible to the everyone around the world. The chapter emphasises the importance of understanding and addressing behavioural issues in dogs through proper training and guidance, rather than resorting to medication.

1 Medication vs. Behavioural Training: Emily expresses her concern about the over-reliance on medication to address dog behavioural issues. Andrew agrees, noting that while veterinarians are experts in medical issues, they might not be equipped to handle complex behavioural challenges.

2 George's Vision: Andrew shares George's vision of expanding their program to train more behaviourists. George is also developing a computer program to provide immediate guidance to dog owners worldwide.

3 Dog Leadership Help Program: George's online program, accessible at www.DogLeadershipAcademy.com, is designed to assist dog owners with behavioural questions. It's a **free tool** that encapsulates George's vast knowledge, offering users the experience similar to consulting with George directly.

4 Community-Based behaviourists: George's ultimate dream is to have dog behaviourists in every community using a leadership based training model, focusing on serving their local areas and ensuring dogs receive the right kind of help.

16

The Panacea

The next day, the morning sun bathed the facility in a golden hue as I arrived. The air vibrated with the familiar sounds of dogs barking and playing. As I stepped out of my car, Andrew was already there, holding onto a lead attached to Millie, the German Shepherd we had rescued just yesterday.

Andrew's gaze met mine, a challenging glint evident. "Ready to work with Millie today?" he inquired, gesturing toward the attentive dog.

I hesitated for a split second, then retorted with a mix of surprise and determination, "Think I can handle Millie? You know…she's supposedly human aggressive."

Andrew's lips curled into a smirk, amusement dancing in his eyes. "Congrats, kid. You've dinged." I chuckled, recognizing the online gaming reference. It was his quirky way of acknowledging my progress, signalling that he believed I was ready for this new challenge.

Feeling a surge of pride and anticipation, I responded, "Alright, let's do this, though, you really should figure out a better nickname for me. And, just because I'm older than you, it better not be 'Grandma.'"

We both chuckled as we entered the training area and Andrew handed Millie's lead to me. My entire focus was on Millie. As I prepared to execute a brace, I tried to recall all the techniques I had been taught, yet something felt off, especially with my stance.

Andrew, ever observant, began to approach. Without uttering a word, he came closer, adjusting my posture by gently placing his hands on my hips. The touch, purely professional and meant to guide, caught me off guard. A warmth spread across my face, and my heartbeat quickened.

"Better?" he queried, a playful glint in his eyes.

Regaining my composure, I replied, "Yeah, thanks," appreciative of his guidance. I took a deep breath, refocusing on Millie, but the fleeting, unexpected closeness lingered in my thoughts.

As the sun climbed higher, Andrew continued to observe and provide further instruction, especially given my initial hesitance with Millie. "If a dog lunges, it's crucial to know how to protect yourself," he began, his tone firm and comforting.

He moved closer, demonstrating the action. "If Millie lunges at you, use your forearms to pull up," he detailed. To emphasise, he lightly touched my elbow, guiding me to the correct position and setting butterflies to wing in my stomach.

Andrew continued, oblivious to the turmoil he had stirred within me. "Your forearms are stronger than your shoulders. Use them to your advantage," he advised.

I nodded, trying to regain my composure. "Got it," I managed to say, my voice slightly shaky. I took a deep breath, reminding myself to stay focused on the training. But the brief, innocent touches from Andrew had left an indelible mark, and I couldn't help but feel a mix of excitement and nervousness as the session continued.

The sun was relentless as the morning moved to midday. The air shimmered in the heat, sweat dripped down my forehead as I worked with Millie, trying to implement everything Andrew had taught me. The intensity of the session, combined with the emotional rollercoaster from earlier, had drained me.

Andrew checked his watch and called out, "You're done, kid…erh, Emily" he corrected himself. I looked up, grateful for the reprieve. "Please put Millie in A Yard and check the water bowl, then let's chat under the canopy."

After settling Millie, I made my way toward Andrew. He tossed me a bottle of water. Catching it mid-air, I was about to thank him when he shouted with a smirk, "Here's some mana potion! Gotta keep your energy at max, after all."

I chuckled, recognizing another gaming reference. The cool water felt refreshing as I took a sip, and I couldn't help but smile at Andrew's attempt to lighten the mood. The day had been full of surprises, and his playful jest was a welcome end to the intense training session.

I took a moment to catch my breath and watched Millie settle into a nice shady spot for a nap. "Andrew," I began, turning to face him, "I've just realised something. Even for a dog as challenging as Millie, it all starts with the Leadership Walk, doesn't it?"

Andrew looked at me, a hint of pride in his eyes. "Exactly. The Leadership Walk is the foundation. It's where we define the nature of our relationship with the dog. It's not just about walking; it's about communicating. Through the Leadership Walk, we get the dog to submit to our authority and, at the same time, earn their respect."

I nodded. "I had no idea how powerful and transformative the Leadership Walk could be. Most people, including me before all this, just squander the walk. We're either on our phones or lost in our thoughts, not really present with our dogs."

Andrew leaned back on the bench, stretching his legs before him. "That's a part of the problem. The walk is a time to bond, to communicate, to lead. If we're not present, we miss out on that opportunity. Dogs live in the present. To be on the same page as them, we need to be present, as well."

* * *

The road home was a familiar one, a route I had taken countless times. I sang along with my playlist until a call rang through to the car. I glanced at the screen, it was titled Emergency Services. A cold knot of dread formed in my stomach.

With a deep breath, I pulled to the side of the road and answered the call. The voice on the other end was calm and professional as she sent my world into a tailspin. My mother had been rushed to the hospital. The urgency in the nurse's voice was unmistakable. I needed to be there, and fast.

A whirlwind of thoughts raced through my mind. Buddy was with me, and I couldn't leave him in the car. I quickly phoned George as I turned the car around and headed back to Gracie's Haven. George was waiting for me at the front gate. He took Buddy and told me to call him when I knew what was happening.

The drive to the hospital was a blur. My hands gripped the steering wheel tightly, my knuckles white. Every red light felt like an eternity. When I finally arrived, a nurse quickly ushered me to a private room where a doctor waited.

His face was sombre as he shattered my world. My mother, my rock, my anchor, had passed away from a sudden heart attack. Memories of her laughter, her wisdom, her strength swirled in my mind. She had mentioned feeling tired and short of breath recently, but she had brushed it off. She was always so strong and resilient. The idea of her showing any sign of weakness seemed impossible. I had tried to get her to see a doctor but she had scoffed at the idea.

The weight of the news was too much to bear. My legs gave way, and I crumpled to the floor, tears streaming down my face. The room seemed to close in on me, the walls pressing in from all sides. The pain was raw, sharp, and all-consuming. She had been my guiding light, my constant, and now she was gone. The void she left behind was vast and overwhelming.

17

True Obedience

The days that followed were a blur of condolences, arrangements, and a profound sense of emptiness. The funeral was a quiet affair, with a handful of close friends and family gathered to pay their respects. The atmosphere was sombre, and thick with grief. The world outside seemed to continue its usual rhythm, yet for me, everything had changed. The sun seemed less bright, the days colder, and the nights longer.

Still, amidst the overwhelming sorrow, there were moments of solace. George, with his wise and understanding eyes, approached me after the service. "Emily," he began, his voice gentle, "I can't even begin to understand the depth of your pain. But remember, grief is a journey, and you don't have to walk it alone." His words, though simple, carried the weight of genuine empathy.

Andrew, ever a pillar of strength, pulled me into a comforting embrace. "I'm here for you" he whispered, his voice filled with emotion. "Whatever you need, whenever you need it." The warmth of his words, the sincerity in his eyes, provided a small measure of comfort in the storm of my grief.

Buddy became my anchor. His intuitive nature seemed to grasp the depth of my pain, and he responded with an outpouring of compassion that was both touching and comforting. Somewhere, in the past weeks, the tables had turned. Where I had been Buddy's saviour and emotional stability, now Buddy was mine.

Each day, as we went about our training routines, Buddy's unwavering loyalty and affection became my solace. The rhythmic cadence of our walks and the shared moments of concentration during our sessions became therapeutic, offering a respite from my grief. Every night, Buddy spent time curled up in my arms. On nights when the loss felt unbearable and tears flowed freely, Buddy's soulful eyes and gentle presence was a testament to his deep bond with me, a silent promise that he would stand by me through thick and thin.

One evening, as the gentle rustle of leaves played a soft lullaby, I found myself engrossed in a training session with Buddy. The progress he had made was clear. His steps were more synchronised with mine, and his joy warmed my heart. In those moments, amidst the tranquillity of nature and the steadfast love of Buddy, I felt a glimmer of hope, a promise that, with time, healing would come.

My focus was momentarily broken by the sharp ring of my phone. Glancing at the screen, I recognized Sally's number and promptly answered, "Hey, Sal! How's it going?"

"Hi Emily, I'm checking in… It's been a few days, are you okay? Do you need anything?"

"Thank you. I'm adjusting. It just takes time. What's up?" I asked.

"Let's plan a day together, just the two of us. I harvested a tonne of tomatoes from the garden and am making a vat of pasta sauce. How about some spaghetti bolognese and cookies afternoon, tomorrow?"

"That sounds amazing! I'll make garlic butter tonight and stop at the bakery and grab some fresh bread on my way there. See you tomorrow!"

~~~

I parked at the curb in front of Sally's house the next day. Before even opening the door of the car, I could hear Benji barking. Yikes. I grabbed my phone and called Sally. "Hey, Sal, I'm in front of your house and I can hear Benji. What's happening?"

The frustration in Sally's voice was evident, "I'm at a complete loss, Em.

Benji's barking is driving me insane. He's constantly barking at birds during the day and possums at night. The neighbours are starting to complain, and I'm just so overwhelmed by it."

"Alright, Sally, let's break this down. We mentioned before about trying to catch Benji in the act. How's that been working out?"

There was a heavy sigh on the other end. "I've been trying, Em, I really have. But I can't always be here, and even when I do catch him, he just ignores me."

"Okay. What's your approach when he doesn't respond?"

There was a brief pause before Sally admitted, "I usually end up raising my voice, hoping he'll finally get it, or I just throw in the towel because it feels so futile."

I nodded. "Sally, escalating your voice isn't the solution. It might even be exacerbating the situation. And giving up only confuses him further. Look, I'm right here. Let's set this up and use this as a teachable moment, okay?"

"Yes, please! What do I do?"

"Sally, teaching Benji to listen and respect your commands is crucial. There are a few ground rules you need to establish.

"Firstly," I continued, "**never issue a command that you're not willing or able to enforce**. In simpler terms, 'I mean what I say, and I say what I mean.' If you tell Benji 'no,' it has to mean 'no.' It can't sometimes mean 'maybe' or 'I'll let it slide this time.' Consistency is key."

I could see Sally in her front window, now. "So, if I tell him to stop barking and he doesn't, what should I do?"

"You go out there and ensure he stops. It might be helpful to keep him on a leash during these training sessions. Remember, it is about guiding and teaching Benji that his actions are inappropriate. We never use force, threats or anger. This way, you can guide him and correct his behaviour more effectively. It's like setting up a scene in a play. You control the environment and guide him through it. Think of every training session as a staged event. This way, you can provide Benji with timely corrections and guidance. Remember, dogs live in the moment. Your feedback needs to be immediate for him to connect his behaviour with the consequence."

I saw Sally nodding behind the glass. "Here's the thing, Sally," I continued.

"If you follow through on your commands 100% of the time, the natural conclusion for Benji is that disobeying you is never an option. It's about consistency. Consistency teaches Benji that it's pointless to defy or ignore your commands. Remember the success principle we talked about?"

"Yes, the idea that if a behaviour is rewarded, it's likely to be repeated. And what I permit, persists."

"Exactly," I affirmed. "In other words, if Benji can get away with being naughty without any consequences, then he'll continue to act out. But if he knows that every single time he misbehaves, he'll be held accountable, he'll quickly learn not to defy your commands. It's all about setting clear boundaries and being consistent in enforcing them."

Sally took a deep breath, "I get it now, Emily. I need to be consistent and follow through every time. No exceptions. What do we do now?"

"Okay, grab Benji's lead and clip it on him. Then go do something somewhere in the house. In a few minutes, I'll knock on your door. When Benji barks, firmly tell him to stop. Make your way toward him. If he stops, praise him. If he continues barking, pick up the lead, tell him to stop again, and follow through by giving the lead a gentle pop to gain his attention and interrupt his fixation on the door. If he stops, praise him and mark it with a "Yes!". If he continues to bark, pull him into a Leadership Walk until he has no choice but pay attention to you. I'll just hang out at your door. When he's calm, I'll give you a minute and knock again. We can do this as long as it takes. The garlic butter needs to soften, anyway," I quipped.

After a couple repetitions, Benji was quietly sitting by Sally's side as she opened the door to my third knock. With another gentle tug of the leash, Benji was told he wasn't allowed to jump on me as I entered. When I had put the bread and garlic butter on the counter, I turned to give both of them lavish praise plus a hug for Sally and a scritches and pets for Benji. While he was still visibly excited, he stayed sitting and continued to check in with Sally. We chatted for a few minutes until Benji lost interest and went to his pillow.

Within fifteen minutes, we were sitting in Sally's breakfast nook tucking into her delicious meal and crunching on toasted garlic bread.

"Look how calm and well behaved Benji is now."

"Thank you for taking the time to stage that entry with us. I'm so grateful!"

I took a deep breath, ready to share a principle that had profoundly impacted my understanding of relationships, both with dogs and humans. "Have you ever heard of the concept of **Emotional Equity**?"

Sally shook her head, "No, what's that?"

"Imagine it as a bank balance. Every interaction, every training session, every moment of discipline and consistency with our dogs is like making a deposit into this emotional bank. Over time, these deposits accumulate, strengthening our bond and relationship with them. So, when we need to guide or ask something of them, we can draw from this Emotional Equity to ensure they respond."

Sally pondered for a moment, "So, it's about building trust and mutual respect over time?"

"Exactly," I affirmed. "I've seen it with George and his dogs. The bond they share is palpable. His dogs respond to him, not out of fear, but because of the trust and respect built from the Emotional Equity he's invested in them.

"In a more personal analogy, this principle isn't exclusive to our canine friends. It's evident in human relationships too. Consider your relationship with your parents. Your emotional equity with your mum is vastly different from that with your Dad. Just because you deeply respect and love your mum doesn't mean that respect automatically extends to your Dad. Your mum has always been there for you, consistently investing time, love, and care. So, without her even asking, you'd willingly do things for her without question. Because your Dad was always a bit distant, even before they divorced, I rarely even hear you speak of him, yet I bet you have already packed away some of your delicious pasta sauce to bring to your mum, right? It's your unconscious way of reciprocating the emotional equity she has built with you over the years."

Sally nodded, "That's a powerful analogy, Emily. And you're right. I have three big jars put aside for her."

"I knew it." I grinned. "Now, relating this back to dogs, if you're the one consistently training and bonding with Benji, but your partner doesn't engage with him in the same way, Benji won't have the same level of respect or responsiveness to your partner. **Emotional Equity isn't transferrable."**

"It's all about the time and effort we invest, whether it's with our dogs or the people in our lives."

I smiled, "Precisely, Sally. And the more genuine effort we invest, the deeper and more meaningful our relationships become."

Sally leaned back. "You know, Emily," she began, her voice tinged with a hint of frustration, "I've spent so much money and time on those obedience schools, and they never taught any of this principle. It was always about tricks, commands and treats, but never about building a relationship or emotional equity."

I nodded, understanding her frustration. "It's not entirely their fault, Sally. Many of these obedience schools are franchises. They follow a set curriculum, often designed by people who might not have a deep understanding of dog behaviour or leadership, or even have a dog themselves. They're just regurgitating what they've been taught."

Sally sighed, "I thought I was doing the right thing by enrolling Benji in those classes."

I reached out, placing a reassuring hand on her shoulder. "You were doing the best you knew how, Sally. Leadership isn't something that's often taught in these schools. George, on the other hand, has a unique perspective. He's owned and operated companies, led teams, and understands the nuances of leadership. He's been able to translate that knowledge into dog training, which is why his approach is so different and effective."

Sally looked thoughtful, "It makes so much sense when you put it that way. Leadership is about building trust, offering guidance, and being consistent. It's not just about giving commands."

I smiled, "Exactly. And just like with people, dogs thrive under strong, compassionate leadership. It's all about building that bond and trust."

For a complete course on dog leadership, come to www.DogLeadershipAcademy.com.

Chapter Summary

In this chapter, Emily assists Sally in addressing Benji's incessant barking issue. The chapter delves deep into the importance of consistency in training and introduces the principle of 'Emotional Equity' in building trust and a strong bond between the handler and the dog. Emily emphasises that leadership, trust, and consistency are the cornerstones of effective dog training.

1 **Consistency in Commands**: Emily advises Sally to always follow through with her commands and to be consistent in her approach. She stresses that if a command is given, it must be enforced, teaching the dog that defiance is not an option.

2 **Emotional Equity Principle**: Emily introduces the concept of 'Emotional Equity', likening it to a bank balance. By investing time, training, and consistency in their dogs, handlers make deposits into this emotional bank. This built trust and allows handlers to draw from this equity when needed.

3 **Relationship Building**: The chapter underscores the significance of building a relationship with the dog, rather than just focusing on tricks, commands and treats. Emily shares personal anecdotes to illustrate the principle of 'Emotional Equity' in both canine and human relationships.

4 **Leadership in Training**: Emily highlights the difference between traditional obedience schools and George's unique approach, which emphasises leadership, trust, and relationship-building over treats and bribery.

Achieve True Obedience with Your Dog

Download the free *Dog Leadership Training Guide* and discover the proven principles of leadership-based training. Learn how to build trust and respect while fostering true obedience without relying on treats or force. Get your free copy today at www.dogleadershipacademy.com!

18

Impulse Control, Delayed Gratification and Pack Hierarchy

The soft morning light streamed through the curtains, illuminating the room with a gentle glow. The serene ambiance of dawn was punctuated by the familiar chords of Don't Stop Believin' from my alarm. Instead of the urge to hit snooze, I found myself humming along, welcoming the day with a enthusiasm.

Sitting up and stretching away the remnants of sleep, my thoughts naturally gravitated to Buddy, excited to see his whole backside wag as I skip down the stairs toward him. While his lack of early training was evident in every spontaneous leap and bound, he was so much easier to bring into line now. I was excited to polish my techniques with a bit more training today.

Through the past couple weeks of mum's death and settling her affairs, Andrew continued to check in with me, he even brought a big basket of food and treats for me, as well as an even bigger tote box full of food and treats for Buddy. He said there was no reason I need be burdened with thoughts of food shopping and prep while I was dealing with much more important things.

When he called last night, we spoke about Sally and Benji, how I'd staged the correction for Benji's barking, and where I wanted to take my training of Buddy. I mentioned how impressive George and his dogs were, and that I'd like to bring Buddy to that level of calm attentiveness.

"Would you like some hands-on help? I could come over and show you a few techniques," Andrew had suggested.

I had paused, considering the offer. The idea of having Andrew's expertise right in my home was too tempting. "That sounds great," I had finally said, smiling. "I think Buddy and I will both benefit from your guidance."

It was exactly 8am when a rhythmic knock echoed through the hallway. I had been prepared for this moment. I already had Buddy leashed and tethered to my side in anticipation of Andrew's arrival.

Buddy's immediate reaction was instinctual. His ears perked up, and his body tensed. The knock was a challenge, an intrusion, and he responded with a deep growl that quickly escalated into a series of aggressive barks. He tried to lunge toward the door, his protective instincts in full display.

With a firm grip on the leash, I acted swiftly. I braced my stance, popped his lead, and I gave a correction, my voice calm yet assertive, "Knock it off, Buddy." The command was clear, and the expectation was that he would obey. After a brief moment of resistance, Buddy's eyes met mine, and he seemed to understand. I commanded, "Sit," and to my relief, he obeyed, his posture more relaxed but still alert.

I marked his obedience with a resounding "Yes!" rewarding his good behaviour. Once I was sure Buddy was in check, I gave him more warm praise, and we walked together to the door. The sequence of knocks came again, and I recognised it as the opening notes of "Shave and a Haircut - Two Bits." My smile was genuine as I opened the door to reveal Andrew standing there, his posture non-threatening. He stepped inside without a word, deliberately standing sideways, avoiding direct eye contact with both Buddy and me. It was a calculated move, designed to minimise any perceived threat.

I allowed Buddy to approach Andrew, watching closely as he sniffed around him. Buddy's tail began to wag in recognition.

Andrew made his way to the couch, taking a seat, and Buddy, sensing a new playmate, eagerly followed. With a playful nudge and a wagging tail, Buddy tried to engage Andrew in a game, his eyes sparkling with mischief.

IMPULSE CONTROL, DELAYED GRATIFICATION AND PACK HIERARCHY

Chuckling, Andrew gave Buddy a gentle pat, and then turned to me, "Hi, Emily. You mentioned you wanted to work on Buddy's impulse control," he patted his duffle bag, "So let's get started. If you're both well behaved, I brought something nice for both of you to enjoy, later."

"Excellent. I've almost eaten my way through everything in that wonderful basket you brought, I just have a couple packages of biscuits left. Do you want anything before we begin? Water? Tea? Coffee?"

"Maybe later. Let's just get into it. Think of impulse control like… a dam holding back water. The water represents Buddy's urges and desires. Without a strong dam, or impulse control, the water can easily overflow, leading to unwanted flooding behaviours.

"Imagine you're at a buffet, and you see all your favourite dishes. Without self-control, you'd pile up everything on your plate, even if you weren't that hungry. With discipline, you choose wisely, taking only what you can eat. That's what we want for Buddy. For him to think before he acts, to make choices based on understanding rather than pure instinct."

I nodded as Andrew continued, "Emily, there's this fascinating study from Standford University on delayed gratification. Have you heard of it?"

I shook my head, intrigued.

Andrew leaned forward in his enthusiasm, "Researchers conducted a series of experiments with children. They were given a choice: they could have one treat immediately or wait for a short period and receive two treats. It's known as the 'Stanford Marshmallow Experiment.' The idea was to test the kids' ability to delay gratification."

I leaned forward, curious. "And what did they find?"

Andrew's eyes lit up, clearly passionate about the topic. "The results were quite revealing. Children were given a choice. They could have a marshmellow immediately, or if they waited for a while, they would receive a second. While there were lots of factors to the experiment, if we boil it down, the children who could wait for the second treat generally fared better in life. They had better academic achievements, healthier lifestyles, and even better social skills. The ability to delay gratification was linked to improved decision-making in various aspects of their lives.

I pondered this for a moment. "So, you're saying that teaching Buddy to control his impulses now can lead to better decision-making in the future?"

Andrew nodded, "Exactly. It's not just about getting him to behave in the moment. It's about setting him up for long-term success. By teaching him to control his urges now, we're giving him the tools to make better choices in the future."

Andrew's explanation was a massive aha moment for me. The connection between a child's ability to wait for a marshmallow and Buddy's training might seem distant, but the underlying principle was the same. It was a profound realisation, and I felt even more motivated to help Buddy develop this crucial skill.

"So, how do I teach Buddy better impulse control and delayed gratification?"

Andrew thought for a moment, then stood up. "Let's do a demonstration. We'll use the front door as our first exercise." He gestured for me to bring Buddy over to the entrance. "Tell me, what usually happens when you're about to take Buddy out?"

I hesitated, "Well, he gets incredibly excited. As soon as I touch the door handle, he's practically pushing past me to get out."

Andrew nodded, "Alright, let's see it in action." He opened the door. As predicted, Buddy lunged forward, eager to explore the world outside. But before he could make his escape, Andrew swiftly and firmly shut the door, causing Buddy to halt abruptly, a look of surprise evident on Buddy's face.

"The idea," Andrew began, maintaining his position by the door, "is to disrupt his usual behaviour. He needs to understand that bolting out isn't an option." He opened the door again, and as Buddy attempted to rush out, he promptly closed it. This dance repeated a few times until Buddy, looking a tad perplexed, chose to sit and wait, trying to decipher this new game.

"Yes! That's it!" Andrew exclaimed, pointing at Buddy's decision to sit. "Good boy!" he exclaimed, love evident in his voice.

I smiled, impressed by the swift change. "So, you're teaching him that patience and waiting for your cue gets him what he wants?"

"Exactly," Andrew affirmed, handing the leash back to me. "And this principle isn't just for the door. It can be applied to various situations. Buddy has been operating on an 'open invitation' basis. We're transitioning him to an 'invitation only' mindset. This means waiting for your signal, whether it's entering a room, jumping on the couch, going out of the crate or greeting guests."

The demonstration was a revelation. By teaching Buddy to wait for an invitation, I was not only instilling patience, I was also fostering a deeper bond of mutual respect between us.

The atmosphere in the room shifted as Andrew turned his attention to the next lesson: impulse control related to food. Buddy, sensing another activity was about to begin, wagged his tail in anticipation, his eyes darting between Andrew and me.

Andrew began by fetching Buddy's food bowl, its metallic sheen reflecting the room's ambient light. "Food is a primary motivator for dogs," he began, his voice steady and instructive. "Teaching them impulse control around it can be one of the most effective lessons."

I handed Andrew the bag of Buddy's kibble, watching intently as he began to fill the bowl. The sound of the kibble hitting the metal echoed slightly, and Buddy's ears perked up, his attention laser-focused on the bowl.

Instead of immediately placing the filled bowl on the ground, as I usually did, Andrew held it firmly in his hands, locking eyes with Buddy. "First, we set the expectation," he explained. He commanded Buddy to sit, his voice firm, not harsh.

Buddy, eager for his meal, complied. His obedience was soon tested as Andrew began to very slowly lower the bowl toward the ground. The moment Buddy's hindquarters lifted off the floor in anticipation, Andrew swiftly raised the bowl back to chest level. This dance of lowering and raising continued, each time Buddy's patience being tested a little more.

I watched, fascinated, as Buddy began to understand the game. His eyes, usually so eager and impatient, now held a glint of determination. He remained seated, even as the bowl was lowered all the way to the ground.

Andrew's lesson wasn't over. Instead of allowing Buddy immediate access to the food, he placed his hands around the bowl, creating a barrier. His posture was assertive, his energy radiating a clear message to Buddy to wait.

Buddy, to my astonishment, didn't lunge or whine. He simply sat, his gaze shifting between Andrew and the bowl, waiting for the next cue. His big beautiful head tilted as he was figuring out the rules of the new game. Andrew's energy was tangible as he projected a silent force field around the food.

After what felt like an eternity, Andrew finally stepped back, giving Buddy a nod of approval. "Okay," he said softly, granting Buddy permission.

Buddy approached the bowl and began eating, his tail wagging in contentment. I was in awe. The transformation, the respect, the patience – it was all so evident in that simple exercise.

Andrew turned to me, his eyes gleaming with a mix of pride and mischief. "Impulse control, Emily. It's all about setting those clear boundaries and expectations. When they get what you're asking of them, they're more than happy to play along. All these little moments, they stack up, helping Buddy learn to respect you more."

We watched Buddy enjoy his kibble for a moment before Andrew announced, "I'm hungry. I brought sandwich fixings." He opened his duffle and produced a series of containers with cold cuts, cheese, sliced tomatoes, lettuce, condiments, and bread. Together, we stacked together a couple of sandwiches. I turned to the cupboard to bring out plates, and by the time I'd turned back, instead of sitting at the dining table, he had plopped down on the floor, cross-legged, and begun to eat. Deliberately, he left a piece of the sandwich on a napkin, tantalisingly close to Buddy, setting up yet another lesson in impulse control.

I watched the scene unfold as I stood by the counter nibbling on my own sandwich. Buddy, with his ever-present appetite, began inching closer to the sandwich, his nose twitching with anticipation. Instead of Andrew pulling the food away or guarding it, he did something I hadn't quite expected. He growled, a deep, resonant sound that seemed to come from the very core of his being.

At the same time, his hands and body language conveyed a clear message to Buddy, "This is mine. Respect that." It was a display of leadership, not dominance in a threatening sense, yet a clear boundary setting. To my surprise, Buddy immediately backed off, sitting down with a slightly sheepish look, his gaze still lingering on the sandwich but clearly understanding the boundary that had been set.

I reflected on human behaviour. If I were enjoying my dinner and someone tried to snatch it away, I'd probably react defensively, maybe even slap their hand away. It's considered rude for someone to take another's food without permission. In the same vein, Andrew was teaching Buddy about respect and boundaries.

Andrew's approach might be perceived by some as being dominant, or even threatening. In reality, he was simply setting clear boundaries, much like we do in our human interactions. It was a lesson in mutual respect and understanding, the unspoken rules that dictate behaviour. Andrew continued eating, seemingly unperturbed by the brief interaction, but the lesson wasn't lost on me. It was a powerful demonstration of leadership and the importance of clear communication.

Andrew, sandwich still in hand, looked up at me with a mischievous glint in his eyes. "You know," he began with a smirk, "they say pack theory has been debunked. But I guess they forgot to tell the dogs that. Besides, dogs don't know how to read research papers."

I chuckled. Buddy was now sitting patiently a few feet away from Andrew, and it was evident that there was a method to Andrew's madness.

"The purpose of that exercise wasn't just to keep my sandwich safe," he said with a playful grin. "It was to teach Buddy about impulse control. It's about teaching him to be respectful of other people's food and boundaries. More importantly, it's about establishing respect."

He paused, taking another bite of his sandwich before continuing. "In the wild, pack order is essential for survival. While domesticated dogs aren't in the wild, those instincts are still very much present. By demonstrating that I'm the leader, Buddy learns to respect me. It's not about fear, it's about understanding roles and hierachy."

I nodded. It was clear that Andrew's methods, while unconventional to some, were rooted in a deep understanding of canine behaviour. The dynamics of the pack, the importance of leadership, and the need for clear boundaries were all essential components of a harmonious relationship between humans and dogs.

We spent the next few hours running through drills, staging events where Buddy was set up for success and given all kinds of love and praise. Andrew reached into his duffle and brought out a Kong toy for Buddy. We ended with a bit of catch in the backyard with the new toy to reward Buddy for an excellent day of work. Soon, Buddy was curled up on the grass between Andrew and myself, on his back, luxuriating in belly rubs.

"Ahhhhh, that was a good day's work." Andrew stood up, stretching his tall frame. "I'm hungry," he declared. "I don't often come to this part of town, and there's this Vietnamese place around the corner that serves an amazing pho soup. George introduced me to it. Fancy joining me?"

I blinked, taken aback. Was this... an invitation? A date, even? The thought sent a flurry of butterflies through my stomach. I had spent so much time with Andrew in a professional setting that the idea of a casual outing felt foreign, yet exciting.

"Sure," I replied, trying to sound nonchalant. "I've never tried pho before."

Andrew grinned, leading the way out of the house. "It's spelled P-H-O, but George told me it's pronounced 'fur' in Vietnamese. Trust me, you're in for a treat."

As we approached the restaurant, the tantalising aroma of spices and herbs wafted through the air. The eatery was modest, with wooden tables and chairs set up in a cosy arrangement. The walls were adorned with pictures of Vietnam, transporting us to the bustling streets of Southeast Asia and the serene landscapes of the Mekong Delta.

We took a seat, and Andrew wasted no time in ordering two bowls of pho. As we waited, the muffle of conversation around us created a warm, inviting atmosphere. Families laughed together, friends chatted animatedly, and the clinking of spoons against bowls added to the symphony of sounds.

When our pho arrived, I was immediately struck by its presentation. A steaming bowl filled with clear broth, tender slices of beef, and soft rice noodles, garnished with fresh basil and bean sprouts. Andrew showed me how to add the accompanying lime, hoisin sauce, and chilli to taste.

IMPULSE CONTROL, DELAYED GRATIFICATION AND PACK HIERARCHY

With my first sip of the broth, the flavours danced on my tongue – a harmonious blend of savoury, sweet, and spicy. The beef was tender, the noodles perfectly cooked, and the fresh herbs added bursts of flavour with every bite.

As we ate, Andrew shared stories of his adventures with George, the places they'd been, and the dogs they'd trained. The meal became more than just food, it became an experience, a journey through flavours and stories.

By the time we finished, the sun had set, casting a soft glow over the streets. We left the restaurant with full bellies and contented hearts, grateful for the shared experience and the delicious taste of Vietnam that had brought us closer together.

As we turned the corner of my street, I slyly inquired, "Remember that Fortnite challenge you were so confident about the other day?"

Andrew chuckled, running a hand through his hair. "Oh, I remember."

"You ready to get schooled?" I said. Issuing the challenge that I knew he could not refuse. His ego would not allow him to back down.

"Alright. It's on! Set up the game, I'll take Buddy out back."

He returned with Buddy, both of them flopping onto the couch. I grabbed a second controller and tossed it to him. "Let's see what you got."

He caught the controller effortlessly, shooting me a cocky grin. His eyes held on to mine a fraction of a second longer than usual… or was that my imagination?

As the game loaded, we settled into the couch, eyes glued to the screen. The familiar Fortnite music played signalling the start of our match.

"Alright," I began, my fingers dancing over the buttons, "let's see if you can back up that bravado."

Andrew smirked, manoeuvring his character with skill. "Trust me, I've got this."

The room was dimly lit, the soft glow from the TV screen illuminating our faces. I could feel Andrew's competitive spirit emanating from him, but I was confident in my skills.

"Ready?" I teased, glancing over at him with a smirk.

Andrew rolled his eyes, gripping his controller. "Just start the game already!"

As the match began, it was immediately evident that I was on a different level. My character moved with precision, dodging bullets and building structures with ease. Andrew, on the other hand, struggled to keep up. Every time he thought he had me cornered, I'd outmanoeuvre him, taking him out with a well-placed shot.

After the third consecutive headshot, I couldn't help but gloat. "Having trouble keeping up, kid," I taunted?

Andrew grunted in frustration, his fingers flying over the controller buttons. It was clear he was outmatched. After another swift defeat, he threw his controller on the coffee table, his face a mix of disbelief and annoyance. He stared at the screen in disbelief. "What the heck?! How are you so good at this?"

I leaned back, a satisfied grin on my face. "I might have forgotten to mention that I'm ranked as one of the top players in the world," I said casually.

Andrew's eyes widened in surprise. "You're kidding," he said, clearly taken aback.

I shook my head, enjoying the moment. "Nope. Looks like you underestimated me. Kid." Emphasising the "kid" to rub it in.

Andrew let out a low whistle, his cocky demeanour replaced by genuine admiration. "Well, colour me impressed," he said, offering a sheepish smile. "Guess I've got some practising to do."

I chuckled, patting him on the back. "Don't feel too bad, kid. You're not the first, and you certainly won't be the last, to be schooled by me."

Chapter Summary

In this chapter, Emily and Andrew delve deeper into the principles of dog training, focusing on impulse control and establishing leadership. Through various exercises, including food control and door manners, Andrew demonstrates the importance of setting clear boundaries and expectations for dogs. The chapter also touches on the dynamics of pack behaviour and the significance of understanding canine instincts.

Key Concepts:

1. **Impulse Control**: Teaching dogs to control their urges, especially in situations that excite or tempt them, is crucial for their overall behaviour. This can be practiced through exercises like waiting patiently for food or not bolting out the door.
2. **Leadership and Dominance**: Dogs have inherent pack instincts. Establishing oneself as a leader, not through fear but through respect and understanding, is essential for a harmonious human-dog relationship. Good leadership is different to dominance through threats or violence.
3. Delayed Gratification: Just because the dog can, does not mean they should act. Be it running out the door, eating or even getting on the couch. Change the rule from being an "open invitation" paradigm to a "invitation only" paradigm to establish a more respectful dynamic in the relationship.
4. **Consistency**: Whether it's in commands or in setting boundaries, being consistent is key. Dogs thrive under clear and consistent guidelines.
5. **Understanding Canine Instincts**: Recognizing and respecting the natural instincts of dogs, such as pack dynamics, can greatly aid in training and establishing leadership.

For more resources, guides, videos and personal coaching come to
www.DogLeadershipAcademy.com

Use Phone to Scan QRCode

19

Fight or Flight - Dog Reactivity and Fear Based Aggression

A few weeks later...

The sun cast sharp shadows on the ground as Buddy and I approached Gracie's Haven. The distant barking of dogs grew louder, signalling our arrival. George, recognizable by his signature cap, stood in the training area.

"Morning, George," I greeted, trying to sound more confident than I felt. "Are we working on Buddy's reactivity today?"

George nodded, his gaze fixed on Buddy. "Yes. How has he been on your walks?"

I observed Buddy closely, his every movement, every twitch of his ears. "We've come a long way."

George nodded, guiding us to a shaded spot. "Absolutely. But remember, Buddy's history as a backyard dog deprived him of crucial early socialisation experiences. This lack of exposure during his formative months now manifests in his reactions. While he is much better than when you first brought him home, each new experience could trigger reactivity. He's a strong boy, you must always be aware of him while out in public."

George leaned against a tree, "Emily, let's talk about the Fight or Flight mechanism. Fight or Flight is an ancient and instinctual response that all animals, including humans, have developed as a means of survival.

"Imagine you're walking in the woods and suddenly come across a bear. Your heart rate increases, your senses sharpen, and adrenaline floods your system. In that split second, your body prepares you to either stand your ground and fight, or to run away as fast as you can. That's the Fight or Flight response in action."

I nodded, picturing the scenario.

George continued, "When Buddy sees another dog, especially in an unfamiliar environment, his body goes through the same rapid changes if he perceives the other dog as a potential threat. Now, if he were off-leash in an open field, he might choose to run away or avoid the other dog – that's the 'flight' part. But when he's on a leash, his options are limited. He can't flee, so he feels cornered, and when an animal feels cornered, it often chooses to defend itself, even if there's no real threat – that's the 'fight' response."

He smiled down at Buddy and scratched behind his ears. "It's not that he's inherently aggressive; he's just reacting based on his instincts and past experiences. Our job is to help him understand that not every dog or situation is a threat, and to give him the tools to respond appropriately."

I frowned, piecing it together. "So, in his mind, other dogs are threats?"

"They can be. It's difficult to know what he may perceive as threatening. It could be the size, the colour, or the posture of the other dog that shifts it into threat or no threat. The good news is, we can help him manage those perceptions. Through consistent training and positive experiences, we can reshape Buddy's perceptions and teach him that he doesn't need to be on the defensive all the time and not all dogs are out to get him."

Throughout the day, George introduced Buddy to controlled encounters with other dogs, ensuring each interaction was positive and under Buddy's threshold. With every success, my hope for Buddy's progress grew.

"So far, so great! Are you ready for a challenge?" George signalled to Andrew. "Hey Andrew, bring Millie out!"

I remembered Millie, the once-aggressive German Shepherd that Andrew had worked with. As Millie appeared, calm and focused on Andrew, I was amazed at her transformation.

George took Buddy's lead and began to walk him toward Millie. I held my breath as Buddy's attention fixed on Millie. I saw the familiar tension in Buddy's body, yet George's swift intervention kept Buddy from fully reacting. Every time Buddy would start to fixate on Millie, George would turn around and lead Buddy away from the perceived threat of Millie, essentially teaching Buddy that he can run away from the threat.

Watching the scene unfold, I realised what George was doing. "You're using the 'level up' approach, right? Keeping Buddy under threshold and exposing him to Millie gradually?"

George nodded, a hint of a smile playing on his lips. "Exactly. We're not trying to flood Buddy with stimuli and hope he copes. We're methodically increasing his exposure, ensuring he remains in a state where he can learn and adapt. Over time, with consistent training, Buddy will learn that seeing another dog, even one as imposing as Millie, doesn't warrant an aggressive response, and he can just walk away. I also rewarded him with positive praises for his success to encourage him that running away and following is rewarded."

The session continued, with George skillfully managing Buddy's reactions, ensuring each encounter was a positive learning experience. With every successful interaction, George would mark Buddy's behaviour with a loving, "Yes!" followed by his genuine praise and love. This was a true master at work in his craft.

It is all coming together. While I see other dogs at large as normal, to Buddy, he is experiencing what I would describe as a crisis and a potential meltdown. In such a crisis, he would normally act out as his instincts dictate, but due to George's timely and swift guidance, Buddy is deferring to George's leadership and allow himself to be lead to safety.

As I took Buddy's lead and began the dance, it occurred to me how effective training beneath tolerance for reactivity was. Buddy had spent his first formative years building a specific way of reacting when he encountered other dogs. It was a set of behaviours deeply etched into his psyche, formed through countless experiences and reactions. This was Buddy's survival mechanism, his way of navigating through the world, even if it was based on misconceptions or overreactions.

Now, as we trained Buddy, I could see how this process was gently rewriting Buddy's ingrained script. It wasn't about stifling Buddy's instincts or punishing him for reacting. Instead, George was methodically and compassionately introducing a new way of thinking, a new protocol for Buddy to adopt.

The brilliance of George's method lay in its simplicity. He wasn't demanding Buddy to confront or challenge the other dog. Instead, he was showing Buddy an alternative, a path of lesser resistance. Through his actions, George seemed to be telling Buddy, "When you see another dog, you don't need to react aggressively. There's another way. You can simply walk away." This approach is significantly different than the treat based approach which relies on using the treats as either a distraction or a desperate bribe to get the dog to focus on the treats rather than the other dog.

> *If you're interested in a step-by-step video guide on how to address dog reactivity and many other behavioural challenges, we've got you covered. Head over to www.DogLeadershipAcademy.com. There, you'll find a comprehensive library of resources, tutorials, and guides designed to help you and your dog.*

"True dog training," I continued, "is more than teaching commands or tricks. It's about reshaping perceptions, changing old narratives, and offering new perspectives. It's about giving dogs like Buddy a fresh start, teaching them that they have choices, that they can opt for calm over chaos."

The afternoon flew by with more challenges and successes. By the time we wrapped up, the sky was painted with shades of pink and purple and Buddy and I practically floated to the car on the winds of achievement.

As Buddy and I approached the car, though, my elation was quickly dampened when I noticed a flat tyre. "Well, I guess I'm changing a tyre in the dark, Buddy."

Footsteps crunched on the gravel behind me and Andrew peered over my shoulder into the spare tyre well. "Oof. Is your spare tyre flat? Look, if you haven't anything pressing tomorrow, I can give you a lift home tonight and a ride back in the morning after we stop at a tyre shop for you. It's way too late to do much tonight."

Gratefully, I nodded, and soon the flat spare tyre, Buddy, and myself were comfortably settled in Andrew's car.

The drive was smooth, and the atmosphere inside the car was light. As we approached my place, Andrew suddenly made a suggestion. "Ever tried Korean barbeque?" he asked, a hint of excitement in his voice. I shook my head, admitting my unfamiliarity with the cuisine. "There's this amazing place nearby. How about we give it a go?"

I hesitated for a moment, my mind racing. Was this a date? Was Andrew interested in me? Pushing all those thoughts aside, my curiosity about the Korean barbeque experience won over, and I agreed.

After dropping off and securing Buddy, we made our way to the restaurant. It was a cosy, authentic setup with wooden tables equipped with built-in grills. The aroma of grilled meats wafted through the air, making my stomach rumble in anticipation. Andrew took the lead, ordering an array of meats, vegetables, and side dishes. Before I knew it, thinly sliced beef, pork belly, and marinated chicken were sizzling on the grill in front of us. The meats were accompanied by a variety of side dishes, including kimchi, pickled radishes, and spicy cucumber salad.

Andrew showed me the ropes, demonstrating how to use the lettuce leaves to make wraps with the grilled meats, adding a dollop of spicy sauce, and a piece of garlic for an extra kick. The flavours were a delightful explosion of sweet, sour, spice, and salt in my mouth - the smokiness of the grilled meat, the tanginess of the kimchi, and the heat of the sauce all melding together perfectly.

As we ate, our conversation flowed effortlessly, ranging from our shared passion for dogs to our favourite travel destinations. The evening was turning out to be quite enjoyable and any initial reservations I had were quickly fading.

When the bill arrived, Andrew swiftly reached for it, insisting on paying. "It was my suggestion, after all, besides, you're not exactly rolling in the money right now." he said with a smile. "You can treat me to dinner after your first paid training gig, okay?"

I couldn't help but chuckle at his chivalry, thinking to myself that if this was indeed a date, it was turning out to be a rather memorable one.

After dinner, Andrew dropped me off at my place, and we exchanged a warm goodbye and an agreed upon time for him to fetch me in the morning.

I let Buddy out, then we curled up together on the lounge. I grabbed my phone and texted Sally, "I think I just went on a date with Andrew."

In less than thirty seconds, Sally's face lit up my screen with her signature ringtone.

"Hey girl! Spill the beans!"

"Sally! Oh my gosh, I don't even know where to begin. Was it a date? Was it not? I'm so confused!"

Sally's laughter echoed through the phone. "Okay, okay, slow down! Start from the beginning."

I recounted the evening's events, from the impromptu Korean barbeque suggestion to the delightful conversation and Andrew's gentlemanly gesture of paying the bill. "And then there's the whole thing with the blonde woman I saw him with. Is he seeing someone? Is he just being friendly with me? I can't figure him out!"

Sally sighed dramatically. "Oh, Em! Men can be so confusing. Honestly, from what you've told me, he seems genuinely interested. And about the blonde? Maybe she's just a friend or a relative. You can't jump to conclusions."

"But he's so… subtle about it," I groaned. "I mean, he's not making any overt moves. No flirty comments, no lingering touches. It's driving me nuts!"

Sally chuckled. "Girl, if he's trying to woo you, he's doing it in the most sophisticated way. He's not coming on strong or being inappropriate. He's taking his time, getting to know you. It's refreshing, actually."

I sighed, running a hand through my hair. "I just wish he'd give me a clear sign, you know? Like, sweep me off my feet or something. This is killing me."

Sally's voice softened. "I get it, Em. But maybe this is his way. Maybe he's being respectful, taking things slow. Maybe he doesn't want things to go weird at your workplace. Give it time. And hey, if he's genuinely interested, he'll make a move. Just enjoy the journey and see where it leads."

I smiled, feeling a bit better. "Thanks, Sal. You always know how to put things in perspective."

Sally giggled. "That's what besties are for! Now, get some rest, and keep me updated. And remember, whatever happens, you're a catch!"

We exchanged a few more pleasantries before hanging up and, as I settled into bed, my mind was a whirl with possibilities.

Chapter Summary

In this chapter, Emily delves deeper into Buddy's training with the guidance of George, focusing on addressing Buddy's reactivity towards other dogs. Through controlled encounters and the 'level up' approach, George demonstrates how to gradually expose Buddy to other dogs, ensuring he remains under threshold and can learn to react positively. The chapter emphasises the importance of reshaping perceptions and offering dogs new options, teaching them that they can choose calm over chaos.

Key Concepts:

1. **Reactivity**: Buddy's background as a backyard dog has led to missed early socialisation, causing him to view other dogs as threats. This results in a 'fight or flight' response when he encounters other dogs.
2. **'Level Up' Approach**: George introduces a method where Buddy is gradually exposed to other dogs, ensuring he remains under threshold. This approach avoids flooding Buddy with stimuli and instead allows him to learn and adapt at a pace that's comfortable for him.
3. **Reshaping Perceptions**: Dog training is not just about commands but

about changing old narratives and offering new perspectives. It's about teaching dogs they have choices and can opt for calm responses. In these controlled encounters, our job is to not only teach Buddy what to do and what not to do, but to guide him to safety and teach him that he can just walk away from anything that he perceives as a threat.

4. **Positive Association**: Just as important as leadership is making the experience a positive one for Buddy. We want to use plenty of praise, happy energy and if possible treats to associate encountering another dog with being rewarded for being calm. This way, Buddy gets to associate getting treats when he sees another dog, but only if he is calm.
5. **Controlled Encounters**: George uses controlled encounters with other dogs to teach Buddy to react positively. By ensuring each interaction is positive and staged to ensure that Buddy's experience is under threshold and stress free, Buddy learns that not every dog is a threat.

We also have a specific guide book that addresses dog reactivity behaviour available at all major book retailers. Look for "The Leadership Guide to Dog Reactivity".

For more resources, guides, videos and personal coaching come to
www.DogLeadershipAcademy.com

Use Phone to Scan QRCode

20

Don't Stop Believing

6am the next day.

The soft morning light filtered through the curtains as the familiar chords of Don't Stop Believin' began to play, gently rousing me from my sleep. As I stretched, I felt the warm, comforting weight of Buddy nestled beside me. His rhythmic breathing and the softness of his fur against my skin added to the serenity of the moment. There's something incredibly special about waking up with a loyal companion by your side; it's a bond that words often fail to capture. The warmth of his body, the gentle rise and fall of his chest, and the trust he placed in me by sharing my bed made the morning even more magical.

Each day, my confidence in my decision to become a full-time dog behaviourist grew. The valuable knowledge and skills I'd acquired over the past few months were shaping me into the professional I aspired to be.

My phone buzzed, breaking my train of thought. It was a message from Andrew letting me know he'd be picking me up soon. I quickly got ready and, before I knew it, Andrew's car pulled up outside. The moment I stepped in, the atmosphere was electric. The radio played hit after hit, and we couldn't resist singing along. From Queen's Another One Bites the Dust to Time After Time by Cindi Lauper, we gave each song our all. Our voices were far from harmonious, often veering off-key, but the sheer joy of the moment made it perfect. We laughed at our own antics, the world outside blurring as we drove.

Upon arriving at Gracie's Haven, Andrew gestured towards my car. "Take a look," he suggested. I hesitated, remembering the deflated tyre from the day before. But, trusting him, I checked and was taken aback to find the tyre perfectly intact and he pulled the repaired spare from his truck. I turned to Andrew, mouth agape. With a playful shrug and a twinkle in his eyes, he simply smiled. After much gratitude and insistence upon repaying him, he reminded me that he expected to be wined and dined once I was a paid behaviourist.

Once through the gates, we focused on more reactivity training with Buddy. Gracie's Haven, with its myriad of rescued dogs, provided the perfect environment for Buddy's training. We spent hours introducing Buddy to different dogs, working on desensitising his reactive tendencies. The progress was evident, and by the end of the day, Buddy's improvement was undeniable.

Andrew, watching from a distance, approached us during a break. "You know," he began, looking thoughtfully at Buddy, "I'm genuinely impressed by how quickly he's adapting. It's not just about the techniques, it's the bond you've built with him. That emotional equity you've invested in Buddy is paying off."

As the week progressed, each day with Buddy felt like a new chapter in an unfolding story. Our mornings began with Leadership Walks, followed by training sessions that focused on his reactivity. With every passing day, I could see subtle changes in Buddy's behaviour. His once tense posture began to relax, and the constant alertness in his eyes started to soften.

George noticed Buddy's progress and decided it was time for a new challenge. He introduced Buddy to Delenn, one of his rottweilers. I held my breath as they approached each other, memories of Buddy's past aggressions flashing before my eyes. But to my astonishment, after a few cautious sniffs and tentative tail wags, the two began to play. Both dogs went down for a play bow indicating their interest in playing, and then it was on. I let go of his lead, then Buddy was chasing Delenn all over the field. The sight of Buddy, joyfully romping around with Delenn, was enough to bring tears to my eyes.

As I sat on the grass, watching them, a wave of emotion washed over me.

Just a few months ago, Buddy was a shadow of the vibrant dog he had become. He was on the brink of being euthanized, his spirit crushed by circumstances beyond his control. And now, here he was, a testament to resilience, love, and the transformative power of second chances.

The weight of our journey, the challenges we'd faced, and the milestones we'd achieved filled me with an overwhelming sense of gratitude. The warmth of that feeling spread through me, a gentle reminder of the incredible bond we'd forged and the bright future that lay ahead for both of us.

As Buddy and Delenn continued their playful dance, I felt a presence beside me. Turning, I found George smiling. He looked out at the dogs, then turned his gaze to me.

"Emily," he began, his voice carrying a hint of emotion, "I thought you'd want to know. Andrew's decided to adopt Millie."

Millie, the once-aggressive German Shepherd who, like Buddy, was on the brink of a tragic end, had found a forever home with Andrew. At this great news, tears welled in my eyes. The transformation of these dogs, from being lost and broken to finding love and purpose, was nothing short of a miracle.

George continued, "It's incredible, isn't it? How love, patience, and a little bit of faith can change destinies."

I nodded, struggling to find words. The magic of this place, the transformations that occurred here, was awe inspiring. It wasn't just about training dogs; it was about healing souls, both canine and human. The facility was a sanctuary, a haven where broken spirits were mended and given a second chance at life.

Overwhelmed with gratitude and the sheer beauty of the moment, I turned to George, wrapping my arms around him in a tight embrace. "Thank you," I whispered, my voice choked with emotion. "For everything."

George patted my back gently, his own eyes glistening. "We're all family here," he murmured. We sat down, watching the dogs play. Second chances, love, and the belief that every soul, no matter how broken, deserved a shot at happiness, those were the important things in life.

After a spell, George turned to me. "Emily, there's a client in town with a reactive dog. I've been thinking... I want you to take this one."

I blinked in surprise, trying to process his words. "Me? But George, that's income for the facility..."

He raised a hand to stop me. "I've seen your progress, not just with Buddy but with all the dogs you've worked with. You've got a gift, Emily. And it's time you start using it more independently."

I swallowed hard, emotions swirling within me. "But what if I mess up? What if I can't handle it?"

George smiled, his eyes crinkling at the corners. "That's where Andrew comes in. I've asked him to act as your coach for this job. He'll be there to guide you, if you need it, but I want you to take the lead."

George's trust in me was both exciting and scary. This wasn't just a job he was handing over, it was a testament to his faith in my abilities. Tears pricked my eyes as gratitude welled up inside me.

"George," I began, my voice shaky, "I can't thank you enough. This means so much to me."

He smiled, patting my back. "Go get 'em, Emily."

After a long day, I stepped out of the training facility with Buddy on our way home, taking a moment to breathe in the fresh air. My gaze wandered across the parking lot, and I spotted Andrew walking toward his car. Millie, the beautiful German Shepherd, was trotting happily beside him, her tail wagging and her head held high. It was hard to believe that just a few weeks ago, Millie was a broken soul, on the brink of being euthanized. Now, she pranced around like a show dog, full of life and joy.

A smile tugged at my lips as I watched the duo. It was moments like these that reminded me of why I had chosen this path. The transformation of dogs like Millie and Buddy was so inspiring. It was a testament to the power of love, patience, and the right training.

Lost in my thoughts, I almost missed the bouquet of flowers that Andrew was holding. The vibrant colours of the roses, lilies, and daisies caught my eye, and I couldn't help but wonder who the lucky recipient was. I also noticed that he changed out of his work clothes into something nice. My heart fluttered with a mix of hope and curiosity. Was it for someone special? Or perhaps a client? I shook my head, trying to dismiss the budding jealousy that threatened to surface.

As Andrew settled into his car, Millie hopped into the back seat, looking out of the window with an excited gleam in her eyes. The car roared to life, and they drove off, leaving me with a whirlwind of emotions.

"Don't Stop Believin', Emily," I whispered to myself, clutching my bag tighter. The journey with these dogs, and perhaps with Andrew, was far from over. And as the familiar chords of Journey's Don't Stop Believin' played in my mind, I felt a renewed sense of purpose and determination. Every dog deserved a second chance, and I was going to make sure they got it.

Taking a deep breath, I opened the door and Buddy hopped into the back seat, his tail thumped against the seat back. As I buckled him in, I bent down to give him a reassuring pat. "Come on, boy, let's go home."

During the drive home, I couldn't release the image of Andrew from my mind. Once Buddy and I had settled in at home, I called Sally's number. She picked up after just two rings. "Hey, Em! What's up?"

I sighed, "You won't believe what I just saw. Andrew, dressed all nice, holding a bouquet of flowers. And he looked… I don't know, different? Like he was on his way to something special."

Sally's voice was teasing, "Ooh, someone's got a crush! Girl, I didn't know you cared so much. Are you falling for him?"

I groaned in frustration, "I don't know, Sal. It's just… I've been hurt before, you know? The thought of opening up again, of being vulnerable, it terrifies me."

Sally chuckled, "Based on your description of him, he sounds like a great guy. Maybe you should let him know."

"I probably should, yet there are so many mixed messages. Urggg…"

Sally's laughter rang in my ears, "Oh, honey, you've got it bad! I hear your concerns, though if you like him, you should let him know. Life's too short for what-ifs."

I sighed, "It's not that simple, Sal. We work together. What if things got awkward?"

Sally was thoughtful for a moment, "Look, Em, I get it. Sometimes, you've got to take a leap of faith. And who knows? Maybe he feels the same way.

And, if he doesn't, then you know, you can emotionally move from there straight to my living room which is stacked with sappy movies and a box of tissues. At least you'll have your answer."

Biting my lip, grateful for Sally's unwavering support. "Thanks, Sal. I'll think about it."

After hanging up, my gaze drifted to Buddy who had sidled up to me, leaning heavily against my leg. Our eyes locked, and a surge of warmth enveloped me. There he was, my steadfast companion, always loyal and protective. Those deep brown eyes always radiated such affection and unwavering devotion. In that moment, I felt an overwhelming sense of gratitude. We may not have much, but we have each other.

Take Your Training to the Next Level

Don't stop here—unlock even more tools and insights to help you transform your relationship with your dog! Visit **www.dogleadershipacademy.com** to download your **FREE** copies of the *Beyond Treats Companion Workbook* and the *Dog Leadership Training Guide*.

What You'll Get:

Beyond Treats Companion Workbook
A free step-by-step guide to help you put the principles of *Beyond Treats* into action:

- **Practical Exercises**: Leadership walks, marker training, impulse control, and more.
- **Daily Checklists**: Stay on track with easy-to-follow tasks.
- **Progress Trackers**: Monitor your improvements and celebrate milestones.
- **Two-Week Plan**: A structured program for immediate and lasting

results.

Dog Leadership Training Guide

The perfect resource for readers who want a deeper dive into the science and principles behind leadership-based training:

- **Expanded Insights**: Explore the psychology of respect and trust in dog training.
- **Structured Manual Format**: Traditional, easy-to-digest explanations of leadership techniques.
- **Comprehensive Understanding**: Learn *why* the methods work, not just *how* to do them.
- **Practical Applications**: Gain confidence in addressing problem behaviors and leading with calm authority.

Visit www.dogleadershipacademy.com **today** to download both FREE resources and take the next step toward building a respectful, harmonious bond with your dog.

21

The First Client

The sun was high, casting sharp shadows on the training ground. I took a deep breath, gearing up for my first client. I really wanted to nail it. Beside Andrew, Buddy sat calmly, his attention fixed on me as I prepared. It was hard to believe that this was the same dog who, just a few months ago, would have lunged at any dog that came his way.

The client arrived, their dog straining at the leash, eyes locked onto Buddy. I could see the tension in the owner's body, their grip on the leash, white-knuckled. Taking a deep breath, I approached them, introducing myself and explaining the process.

"We'll start with the Leadership Walk," I began, demonstrating the brace routine. "This will help establish your leadership and control."

As we walked, I could see the client struggling to maintain control as their dog lunged and barked. Changing tacks, I introduced them to the "Where Do You Think You're Going" routine and demonstrated how to brace, pivot and change direction to refocus the dog's attention.

The client tried it, and after a few attempts, their dog started to respond, looking to them for guidance instead of fixating on Buddy.

Next, we focused on teaching the dog to disengage from potential conflicts. "Rather than reacting, we aim for him to learn the art of disengagement and walking away," I articulated, guiding the client meticulously through each step.

Throughout our session, I was acutely aware of Andrew's observant gaze. Yet, to my astonishment, he remained mostly hands-off, chiming in occasionally with words of encouragement and sage advice. Most impressively, Buddy was the epitome of composure. Not once did he retaliate, even when the client's dog lunged at him. Instead, he kept his focus on Andrew, at one point even rolling onto his back for a delightful scratch, signalling to the other dog his peaceful intentions and lack of desire for confrontation.

By the session's conclusion, the client's dog exhibited a marked change, seeking guidance from its owner rather than succumbing to impulsive reactions. The owner too radiated newfound confidence, standing taller and holding the leash with a sure grip. I reviewed what we had covered, made a plan for their homework, and we exchanged phone numbers so we could stay in touch as questions arose.

As the client left, thanking me profusely, I felt a rush of pride and satisfaction. I had done it. I had taken all the knowledge and skills I had learned and applied them successfully. And Buddy, my faithful companion, had been the perfect partner, calm and unreactive even in the face of provocation.

Andrew approached, a smile playing on his lips. "You did good, Emily." he said, raising a hand for a high five. "Really good." Leaning down, he gave Buddy a kiss on the head and a loving hug. Conveying his love and pride in Buddy. Buddy beamed at him.

With a wag of his tail and an expectant gaze fixed on me, Buddy elegantly raised his paw, as if extending an invitation for a handshake. I met his gesture with a high five, declaring, "I am so proud of you, Buddy."

I grinned, feeling on top of the world. "Thanks, Andrew. I couldn't have done it without you."

He chuckled. "Maybe, but today, you proved that you can stand on your own two feet. And I couldn't be prouder."

The satisfying weight of the payment in my hand made the day's success even sweeter. I felt a sense of accomplishment, not just for handling the client's dog but also for earning a decent sum for my efforts. I turned to Andrew, "My first paid client." I waggled the fan of cash at him. "I owe you a

THE FIRST CLIENT

dinner. How about we celebrate at that local burger shop up the road?"

Andrew's eyes lit up, "Sounds perfect. They have tables outside, so we can take the dogs with us."

We buckled the dogs into his back seat and drove to a classic diner that looked like a scene from Grease or Happy Days. The rear half of a 1950s hot rod was part of the neon sign above the restaurant, there were servers on roller skates whizzing around the outdoor serving area, and the garage doors of the building were open to black and white checkered floors, walls adorned with posters and memorabilia, and a giant jukebox flashing in rhythm with the golden oldies. It was as if we had stepped back in time.

We settled at a table near the doors, secured the leashes, and we soon were sipping milk shakes and nibbling on fries. When the infectious beats of a classic rockabilly song began to play, Andrew popped up and extended his hand to me with a mischievous grin. I hesitated for a split second, then let him pull me onto the dance floor.

With a confident grip, he led me into the rock step swing. I stumbled at first, trying to match his rhythm, but Andrew's lead was strong and sure. After a few basic moves, I began to relax, trusting him to guide me. The dance became a whirlwind of spins, twirls, and laughter. Andrew's skill was evident, he moved with grace and precision, making even the most complex moves look effortless.

As one song transitioned into another and the rhythm shifted, Andrew seamlessly adapted. He guided us into a double step swing, and I matched his movements, somewhat clumsily. As we danced, the world around us blurred, and we became lost in the music and each other's presence.

After the song ended, Andrew walked to the jukebox. He chose "Time After Time" by Cyndi Lauper. Smiling, he extended his hand, inviting me into the dance.

He drew me close, our bodies aligning in the classic box step of the rumba, a dance that whispered tales of Cuban romance, characterised by its sultry hip movements. At first, I stumbled, my steps clumsy and uncertain. Eventually, under Andrew's gentle yet confident guidance, I found myself surrendering to the captivating melody, our feet moving in harmonious rhythm.

The world around us blurred. His every move exuded confidence, but it was his guidance that mesmerised me. With a flourish, he spun me out, only to pull me back into a warm embrace. It felt as if we had been transported into a Disney tale, reminding me of the scene from "Beauty and the Beast."

What struck me most was that Andrew was able to guide me through dance simply with the use of his hands and body without saying a word. It was difficult in the beginning, yet as I relaxed a bit and gradually let go instead of fighting his guidance, we began to move as one.

"Is this what it feels like to be guided in a Leadership Walk? As I gradually adjust to the role of a follower, does a dog also instinctively embrace its role as a follower?" I wondered to myself. It was yet another aha moment in my ongoing learning journey with Andrew.

When the song ended, we returned to our table, breathless and laughing. The evening had turned into one of the most memorable nights of my life. As we dug into our burgers, I couldn't help but think how lucky I was to have Andrew by my side, not just as a mentor but as a friend.

As we slurped the last of our shakes, Andrew drew a breath, "Emily, I really enjoy spending time with you. I know we sort of work together, and I don't want to be inappropriate, so just tell me if I'm being too forward. How do you feel about us spending more time together outside of Gracie's Haven?"

I fought down my rising excitement for a moment and looked deeply into his eyes. "Andrew, I need to understand where I stand. I saw you with that gorgeous lady in her zazzy sports car, and then another time all dressed up with a bouquet of flowers. If there's someone else, I would prefer to keep our friendship professional only."

Andrew's brow furrowed a moment, then laughed, "Amanda? She's my sister! And the flowers were for my mum. It was her birthday, so we planned a dinner at Amanda's house to surprise her."

Andrew reached for my hand and I allowed his warm squeeze to reassure me. "I can see how that might have been confusing, and I've been a bit cautious with you."

"Cautious?"

"Yes, well," Andrew looked a bit sheepish. "I admire you, and I don't want to ruin our working relationship. It's just been amazing watching you learn and grow in confidence. And, outside of that Fornite humiliation, you've been incredibly fun to be around."

I laughed. "I see. You've done such a great job training me with Buddy, maybe I can share a few pointers in the game so you stand a chance of keeping up with me."

"I look forward to it! Perhaps you and Buddy would like to come over to my place for dinner tomorrow night? I feel I need to start my Fornite training immediately." He squeezed my hand and his smile melted my knees.

Chapter Summary

In this chapter, Emily takes on her first client, applying the dog training techniques she's learned to help the client's reactive dog. With Buddy by her side as a model of calm behaviour, Emily successfully guides the client through Leadership Walks and teaches them how to redirect their dog's attention away from triggers. The chapter emphasises the importance of leadership, control, and consistency in dog training.

Key Concepts:

1. **Leadership Walk**: Emily introduces the Leadership Walk to the client as a foundational exercise. This technique helps establish the handler's leadership and control over the dog.
2. **Brace Routine**: Emily demonstrates the brace routine, emphasising its role in establishing leadership during walks. By forming a proper brace, it prevents the handler from being yanked or hurt by a dog who pulls.
3. **Redirecting Attention**: When faced with distractions or triggers, Emily teaches the client to pivot and change direction and leading the dog away from the stressor, refocusing the dog's attention on the handler instead of the triggering stimulus like another person or dog.
4. **Walking Away from Conflic**t: Emily emphasises the importance of

teaching the dog to disengage and move away from potential conflicts, rather than reacting impulsively.

5. **Trust in Training**: Emily reflects on the dance with Andrew, drawing parallels between the trust required in dance and the trust needed in the handler-dog relationship. Submitting to a leader is not necessarily a sign of weakness. Each person has a role to play and understanding their roles make moving forward, much like in dancing, more harmonious together.

22

The Barker

Weeks later.

The days following the completion of my studies with George were a whirlwind of activity. With the knowledge and skills I had acquired, I had earned my certificate of completion and I felt ready to embark on my own journey. I began to implement the marketing strategies he had taught me, posting heartfelt messages about the bond between dogs and their owners, the challenges they face, and the solutions I could offer.

It wasn't long before my phone started buzzing with notifications. Emails, messages, and calls began pouring in. People reached out, sharing their stories, their struggles, and their hopes for their beloved pets. It was evident that my messages had struck a chord. They resonated with dog owners who felt misunderstood, frustrated, and, at times, let down by other well meaning yet less knowledgeable trainers.

I started booking appointments, journeying to homes, parks, and even offices to meet with clients and their four-legged family. With Buddy by my side at each session, we formed a dynamic duo. I would observe, interact, and train, while Buddy often served as a calming presence or a demonstration partner. I paid close attention to the owners, delved deep into their concerns, and then collaborated with their dogs, employing the methods and tactics I had mastered.

The gratitude and relief on the faces of my clients at the end of each session were immeasurable. It was clear that the impact of my work extended beyond just the dogs; I was helping families rebuild trust, understanding, and harmony in their homes.

I had one more appointment that day. I pulled up to the curb of a quaint brick house in a nice suburban neighbourhood. Even before I cut the engine of my car, I heard the panicked barking coming from the backyard.

I was greeted at the door by a middle-aged woman with a worried expression, her name was Linda. Behind her stood a tall man with greying hair whom she introduced as Mark. Their faces were etched with concern and desperation.

"Emily, thank you for coming on such short notice," Linda said, her voice shaky. "This is our last resort."

I nodded. On our phone call, Linda had confessed her neighbours were on the brink of reporting her to the local government for the uncontrolled barking. I calmly reassured her, "I understand how serious this is. I've dealt with similar cases before. Let's see what we can do."

Mark led the way to the backyard where a robust English Staffy was pacing back and forth, barking non-stop at the fence. The dog's name was Bruno, and he had a gleam of manic in his eyes.

"We've tried everything," Mark explained, his voice filled with frustration. "Toys and training. Nothing seems to work. And now, with the threat of the local government, we're at our wits end."

Linda added, "We love Bruno. He's been with us since he was a pup. With the housing crisis, moving isn't an option. And we can't... we just can't bear the thought of putting him down."

I felt the weight of their desperation. The stakes were high, not just for Bruno, but for this family that loved him dearly. I began to assess the situation, determined to find a solution that would save Bruno and bring peace back to this household.

Linda cleared her throat, her voice quivering slightly. "We've tried everything, Emily. The vet said Bruno was anxious and prescribed some anti-anxiety medication. But it hasn't made a difference. He still barks incessantly."

THE BARKER

Mark added, "We love Bruno, but we can't continue like this."

I offering a reassuring smile. "I understand your concerns, Linda, Mark. It's not uncommon for dogs to bark excessively due to various reasons. The good news is, we can address this."

Linda's eyes brightened with a glimmer of hope. "You think you can help?"

"Absolutely," I replied confidently. "First, we need to understand the root cause of Bruno's barking. There are typically four main reasons why dogs bark."

I began to enumerate, using my fingers for emphasis. "One, **lack of exercise and boredom**. Dogs are active creatures, and if they don't get enough physical and mental stimulation, they can resort to barking."

Mark nodded, "That makes sense."

"Two," I continued, "**Property defence**. Dogs are territorial by nature, and they might bark to warn off perceived threats."

Linda interjected, "But our neighbourhood is so quiet."

I nodded, "It could be something as simple as a passing car or other animals like a cat or birds. Three, **demand barking**. This is when a dog barks to get something they want, like attention or food."

Mark chuckled, "Bruno's quite the attention seeker."

"Four, **true anxiety**. This is when a dog feels genuinely threatened or scared."

Linda sighed, "It's so overwhelming. But knowing the reasons helps."

I smiled, "Understanding is the first step. Now, let's work together to address each potential cause and find a solution for Bruno."

I took a moment to observe Bruno. He seemed restless, his eyes darting around, occasionally letting out a soft whine. Turning my attention back to the couple, I inquired, "How often do you walk Bruno?"

Linda and Mark exchanged a guilty glance before Mark admitted, "Not as often as we should. He pulls so hard on the leash, it's become a chore to walk him. So, we mostly leave him in the backyard."

Linda quickly added, "We've given him plenty of toys, though. But he doesn't seem interested in them."

"Having toys in the backyard doesn't automatically cure boredom," I began, trying to find a relatable analogy. "Think of it this way, if simply owning gym equipment was the solution, everyone would be fit, right?"

Linda and Mark looked at each other, then burst into laughter. Mark replied, "That's a good point. We never thought of it that way."

I smiled, "It's all about engagement and interaction. Just like we need motivation to use the gym equipment, Bruno needs motivation and guidance to engage with his toys and environment."

"So, tell me about your relationship with Bruno," I began, looking between Linda and Mark.

Linda's eyes softened as she glanced at Bruno, "He's our baby. We don't have children, so he's everything to us. We dote on him, give him everything he wants."

Mark chuckled, "Yeah, he's spoiled. We can't help it. He gives us those puppy eyes, and we just melt."

I nodded, taking in their words. "Do you feel Bruno respects you both?"

The couple exchanged a knowing look. Mark let out a light laugh, "Respect? Oh no. He rules the roost here. We often joke that we're just living in Bruno's house, serving his every whim."

Linda added, "It's true. He gets his way with everything. If he wants to sit on the couch, he does. If he wants a treat, he gets it. "

I took a deep breath, choosing my words carefully. "Linda, Mark, while it's endearing to treat Bruno like a baby, it's crucial to establish clear boundaries and roles in the house. The current setup, where Bruno gets everything he wants, might seem cute, but it's dysfunctional. It's most likely the root cause of the barking problem."

Linda's eyebrows knit together in confusion. "How so?" she asked, genuinely curious.

"Think of it this way, right now, Bruno sees himself as the prince of this castle," I began, gesturing around the room. "And you both are his loyal servants, catering to his every whim. It's a dynamic that has been established over time, and Bruno has grown accustomed to it."

Mark chuckled, "Well, when you put it that way, it does sound a bit ridiculous."

I smiled, "It's a common scenario in many households. Here's the thing, when you both leave the house, in Bruno's mind, it's like the prince being left without his serving staff. He's understandably upset and demands, through his barking, that his 'servants' return to serve him."

Linda's eyes widened in realisation. "So, all this time, he's been barking because he wants us to come back and attend to him?"

I nodded, "Exactly. It's demand barking. He's used to getting his way, and when something disrupts that routine, he vocalises his displeasure."

Mark sighed, running a hand through his hair. "We've created a little monster, haven't we?"

I chuckled, "Not a monster, just a prince who needs a bit of guidance. With some adjustments and training, we can help Bruno understand his proper role in the household and reduce the barking."

The atmosphere shifted from confusion to understanding as Linda and Mark began to grasp the changes that needed to be implemented for Bruno's well-being and their peace of mind.

"Linda, Mark," I began, "the core issue here is a lack of leadership. In the absence of clear guidance, Bruno has naturally assumed the leadership role in the house. Combine that with his lack of stimulation and exercise, and you have a recipe for the excessive barking you're experiencing."

Mark's face contorted with frustration. "But how do we walk him? He pulled so hard he injured my back."

I smiled confidently, "I understand your concern, Let's take it one step at a time. OK?" Without waiting for a response, I motioned for them to follow me to the backyard.

Bruno perked up, his tail wagged in anticipation. I pulled a slip lead from my pocked, looped it over his head, and began to demonstrate the Leadership Walk technique through a combination of the brace technique and the "Where Do You Think You're Going" methods.

Within just 15 minutes, the transformation was evident. Bruno, who had once been the unruly prince of the house, was now much more docile, tracking and following my every move, his eyes locked onto mine, waiting for the next command.

Linda and Mark watched in stunned silence. Their jaws dropped, and their eyes widened in disbelief. "We've never seen him behave like this," Linda whispered, her voice filled with awe.

Mark nodded in agreement, "It's like he's a completely different dog."

"Addressing the root cause and establishing clear leadership is key. And as you've seen, with the right techniques and consistency, change is not only possible, it can happen quite quickly.

"Through the Leadership Walk, we're teaching Bruno a fundamental lesson: he is to follow, not lead. By doing this, we're re-establishing the natural order in your household. Bruno isn't the prince, he's a cherished member of the family, yes, but he's not in charge. We're restoring both of you, Linda and Mark, to your rightful places on the throne."

Linda nodded slowly, taking in every word. "What you're saying makes so much sense, Emily. It's all very... common sense, really. In our desperation to shower Bruno with love, we inadvertently created this... well, royal monster."

Mark looked down guiltily. "We just wanted to give him the best. He's a rescue dog and his life wasn't very easy before us."

I smiled reassuringly, "Love doesn't mean letting someone do whatever they want. True love is guiding them, setting boundaries, and teaching them. With Bruno, it's about showing him his place in the family hierarchy."

Linda took a deep breath, determination shining in her eyes. "We promise to continue with the Leadership Walk diligently. We owe it to Bruno and to ourselves."

I nodded, "That's the spirit. And remember, you don't need to spend hours on this. Just 15-20 minutes a day is enough. In fact, you don't even need to venture out onto the streets initially. Practice the Leadership Walk in your backyard or driveway. Once you're confident, and Bruno is consistently following your lead, then you can level up and take him out to the street. It's all about gradual progression and setting him up for success.

"The Leadership Walk isn't just about leadership. It's a holistic approach that addresses multiple issues at once. While it establishes respect and leadership, it also serves another crucial purpose: it's both physically and mentally draining for Bruno."

Mark raised an eyebrow, intrigued. "How so?"

I smiled, "Dogs, especially energetic breeds like Staffies, need physical exercise. They also need mental stimulation. The Leadership Walk provides both. When Bruno is focusing on following your lead, he's not just walking, he's thinking and concentrating. This mental engagement, combined with the physical activity, tires him out in the best possible way."

Linda's eyes widened in realisation. "So, it's like a two-for-one deal? We're addressing his need for leadership and his need for exercise and mental stimulation all at once?"

"Exactly," I affirmed. "And when a dog is both physically and mentally satisfied, unwanted behaviours like excessive barking often decrease. Remember, a tired dog is a good dog. By addressing his boredom and lack of exercise through the Leadership Walk, you're tackling the root causes of his barking."

I continued, "And while the Leadership Walk is a great start, there are other ways to keep Bruno engaged and reduce his boredom. For instance, you can provide him with a Kong toy filled with peanut butter or minced meat. If you freeze it overnight, it'll give him something to work on and occupy him for a good while when you're not around."

Mark jotted down the suggestion, looking intrigued. "That sounds like a neat idea."

Linda chimed in, "Anything to keep him busy."

I nodded, "Exactly. And there are also puzzle toys available that require Bruno to figure out how to access the treats inside. It's a great way to stimulate his mind."

Linda looked thoughtful for a moment. "What about putting him in a crate during the day? I've heard about it, but it seems… I don't know… a bit cruel?"

I understood her concerns. "It might seem that way, but think of it from another perspective. If the alternative is considering putting Bruno down because of complaints or if he becomes destructive due to unchecked behaviours, then having him safe and quiet in a crate while you're gone is a much better option. It becomes their safe space, and many dogs actually enjoy the security it provides."

Mark looked convinced, "It's worth a shot. We just want what's best for

Bruno."

Linda nodded in agreement, "We'll give it a try. Thank you, Emily."

I smiled, "I am always here to help. And remember, every dog is different. It's all about finding what works best for Bruno and being consistent with it."

I spent the remainder of my time with Linda, Mark, and Bruno guiding them through exercises, crafting a plan with them, and exacting the promise they'd continue to touch base with me, especially with concerns or new behaviours. I recounted tales of my first days with Buddy and paraphrased George's advice to me, "You can't pity him. Pity will muddy the waters. It's not what Bruno needs."

At the time, I hadn't fully grasped the depth of his words. After seeing situations like Linda and Mark's with Bruno, it became crystal clear. Pitying a rescue, especially in the initial stages, can lead to a lack of structure and discipline. And without that structure, the dog often steps into the leadership role, creating a dysfunctional dynamic in the household.

It's not that rescues don't deserve compassion and understanding. They do. But they also need clear boundaries and consistent leadership. They need to know where they stand, what's expected of them, and that they can trust their human to guide them much like a parent to a child.

Buddy, lying quietly in the back seat for the ride home, seemed to sense my introspection. He let out a soft whine. I smiled, giving him a gentle pat before putting the car in gear. Our bond had grown so strong over the months, a bond built on mutual respect and trust. I thought about how far we'd come, from those early days of uncertainty to the deep connection we shared now.

I realised that George's advice wasn't just about not pitying Buddy. It was about seeing him for who he truly was, understanding his needs, and providing him with the guidance and structure he craved. It was about building a relationship based on mutual respect, trust, and understanding.

Chapter Summary

In this chapter, Emily, armed with the knowledge from her studies under George, begins her journey as a dog behaviourist using George's Dog Leadership techniques. She successfully markets her services, resonating with many dog owners. Emily encounters Linda and Mark, a couple desperate to address their dog Bruno's incessant barking. Through careful observation and assessment, Emily identifies the lack of leadership and stimulation as the root causes of Bruno's behaviour. She introduces the Leadership Walk as a holistic solution, emphasising its role in establishing leadership, as well as providing physical exercise, and offering mental stimulation.

Key Concepts:

1. **Importance of Leadership**: Dogs need clear leadership. In its absence, they might assume the dominant role, leading to behavioural issues such as demand barking and aggressive behaviour.
2. **Leadership Walk**: A technique introduced by Emily, the Leadership Walk teaches dogs to follow rather than lead. It establishes the owner's leadership and provides both physical and mental stimulation for the dog.
3. **Physical and Mental Stimulation**: Dogs require both types of stimulation. Lack of either can result in unwanted behaviours like excessive barking. The Leadership Walk addresses both needs simultaneously.
4. **Addressing Root Causes**: Instead of merely treating symptoms (like barking), it's essential to identify and address the root causes of a dog's behaviour.
5. **Consistency in Training**: Emily emphasises the need for consistent practice, even if it's just for a short duration daily, to see positive changes in a dog's behaviour.

Through her interaction with Linda, Mark, and Bruno, Emily showcases the importance of understanding a dog's needs and the role of leadership in ensuring a harmonious relationship between dogs and their owners.

We also have a specific guide book that addresses separation anxiety and excessive barking behaviour available at all major book retailers. Look for "The Leadership Guide to Separation Anxiety and Excessive Barking".

Ready for More In-Depth Guidance?

If you're looking for a deeper dive into the principles and strategies discussed in this chapter, don't forget to download your **free** copy of the **Dog Leadership Training Guide** at www.dogleadershipacademy.com.

This comprehensive guide offers:

- **Detailed Summaries:** Clear, structured explanations of key concepts.
- **Step-by-Step Instructions:** Practical, easy-to-follow exercises to implement leadership-based training.
- **Expanded Insights:** Understand the *why* behind every method to build confidence in your approach.

Download it **FREE** today and take the next step toward becoming the calm, consistent leader your dog respects and trusts. **Visit www.dogleadershipacademy.com now!**

23

The Insecure Jealous Boyfriend

The sun streamed through the windshield as I drove to my next appointment singing along to familiar songs on the radio. My next client, Janice Umber, had described her dog as human-aggressive, a serious issue that always required a delicate approach. The twist? It was a tiny chihuahua causing all the ruckus.

I parked in front of her house, took a moment to gather my thoughts, and prepared for the session ahead. In the back, Buddy, my trusty wingman, lay quietly. As I stepped out of the car and caught sight of my client, my heart nearly stopped. Standing there was the very woman who had thrown the soup container at my face months ago. Memories of that humiliating encounter flooded back, and for a split second, I considered turning around and driving away. Why should I help someone who had treated me so poorly?

Then, George's teachings echoed in my mind. It wasn't about the client or the money; it was about the dog. If I walked away now, it would be the chihuahua that suffered the consequences. I took a deep breath, pushed my personal feelings aside, and I approached Mrs. Umber with a professional smile.

"Good morning, Mrs. Umber," I greeted, hoping she wouldn't recognize me from our previous encounter. "I'm Emily, the Dog Behaviourist, here to help with your dog."

The warm sunlight cast a soft glow on the suburban street, but the atmosphere was anything but serene. As I approached Mrs. Umber, I could see the dawning recognition in her eyes. The colour drained from her face, replaced by a look of sheer horror. "Oh God, it's you," she whispered, her voice trembling. "I'm so sorry. You must think I am an awful person." Her eyes glistened with tears, and I could see the weight of guilt pressing down on her.

I inhaled deeply as I tried to maintain my composure. "It's okay," I replied, my voice gentle. "I'm here to help. Please, tell me what's happening with your dog." I could see the pain in her eyes, and I remembered George's teachings about compassion and understanding.

Mrs. Umber's voice cracked as she continued, "My dog, Mr. Biggles, had bitten my grandson that day. I was so distraught and overwhelmed. I shouldn't have taken it out on you. I'm not usually like that."

I thought back to that fateful day, the soup, the humiliation, Yet, in a strange twist of fate, that incident had set me on a new path, leading me to George and a newfound purpose. If it hadn't been for Mrs. Umber's outburst, would I still be stuck in that dead-end job, feeling lost and unfulfilled?

With a newfound understanding, I stepped closer and wrapped my arms around Mrs. Umber, offering her a comforting embrace. Pulling back, I looked deep into her eyes, my voice sincere, "I forgive you. In a way, I have to thank you. Because of that day, I found my calling. I'm here today, saving dogs, and it's all partly because of you."

The weight of my words seemed to crash down on Mrs. Umber. The raw emotion, the guilt, the relief – it all became too much for her. Tears streamed down her face as she sobbed uncontrollably, then she suddenly turned on her heels and rushed back into her home.

I stood there, the gentle breeze rustling the leaves around me, feeling a mix of emotions. Compassion, understanding, and a sense of closure. The past had come full circle, and I was ready to move forward. I decided to give Mrs. Umber a moment to gather herself. Buddy and I sat on her front step to wait.

The minutes ticked by as I answered some emails and allowed Mrs. Umber the time she needed to compose herself. Soon, the door behind me opened. Mrs. Umber emerged more composed, holding onto a leash attached to a feisty little chihuahua – Mr. Biggles.

THE INSECURE JEALOUS BOYFRIEND

His tiny frame was a stark contrast to the ferocity he displayed. The moment his eyes locked onto mine, he began barking and lunging, straining against the leash. What struck me more was Mrs. Umber's reaction. Her grip on the leash tightened, her knuckles turning white. Her posture became rigid, her eyes darting nervously between me, Buddy, and Mr. Biggles. She also tried to soothe him, her voice a mix of desperation and hope, "It's OK honey. That's your trainer, Emily. Shh, it's OK." Of course, her words did little to calm the agitated chihuahua. It was evident that she was anticipating his aggressive behaviour, exacerbating the situation with her own anxiety. The tension between them was noticeable, a clear indication of their shared history and the challenges they faced together.

I stood there, observing Mrs. Umber and her pint-sized terror, Mr. Biggles. The contrast between the two was comical. Mrs. Umber, with her refined appearance, and Mr. Biggles, with his fierce demeanour, seemed an unlikely pair.

"I'm truly sorry for earlier," Mrs. Umber began, her voice quivering. "Thank you for being so understanding and professional, especially after... well, everything."

I nodded, my gaze shifting to Mr. Biggles, who was still eyeing Buddy and myself with a level of hatred that seemed disproportionate for his size. Every muscle in his tiny body was taut, ready to spring into action. He stared at me like he was ready to tear a hunk of meat from my ankle.

"This," Mrs. Umber sighed, pointing at the little dog, "is Mr. Biggles."

I couldn't help but smirk a little. "He certainly has an, ummm... big personality for such a small package," I remarked.

Mrs. Umber chuckled, "That's one way to put it. He's been a handful, to say the least."

I sighed inwardly. I had never been a fan of chihuahuas. They always seemed so... neurotic. Like tiny bundles of nerves wrapped in a rat's body. I had to stifle a chuckle.

Mrs. Umber, her eyes filled with hope. "Can you help Mr. Biggles, Emily? I just want him to be happy and well-adjusted."

I smiled reassuringly, "That's what I'm here for, Mrs. Umber."

I looked at Janice, gauging her reaction to my rather bold statement, "You've got an insecure jealous boyfriend."

Mrs. Umber's eyebrows knitted in confusion. "A what? What do you mean?" she asked, her gaze shifting between me and Mr. Biggles.

Taking a deep breath, I began, "Before I explain myself, let me tell you a little bit about my ex." I paused, memories of our tumultuous relationship flooding back. "He was a very insecure, jealous, controlling type. He wouldn't let me go anywhere. I used to go to the gym, and he manipulated me to stop going because he didn't want other men to steal me or talk to me. In his mind, he felt that he owned me."

As I spoke, I noticed Janice's eyes soften, a hint of understanding and empathy appearing. She nodded slowly, her gaze distant. "I was quite a looker in my younger days," she began, a wistful smile playing on her lips. "I had one of those, too."

I tilted my head, intrigued. "Really? So, what did you do? How did you handle that one?"

Mrs. Umber's eyes sparkled with a mix of mischief and pride. "I told him to take a hike," she declared with a hint of defiance. "I told him I wasn't his property!"

I couldn't help but chuckle as an unexpected bond formed between us. "Exactly," I responded, nodding in agreement. "That's what I did to mine, too."

As I observed Mr. Biggles, his tiny frame taut with tension and eyes darting suspiciously, Mrs. Umber followed my gaze. She looked from Mr. Biggles to me, her eyes widening in realisation. "You little ratbag!" she exclaimed, pointing at the feisty chihuahua. She then turned to face me, her expression a mix of disbelief and curiosity. "Is that what is going on here with Mr. Biggles?"

I nodded, choosing my words carefully. "Don't you see? He's guarding you, protecting you from perceived threats, much like an insecure boyfriend would."

Mrs. Umber paused, her eyes thoughtful as she processed my words. She looked down at Mr. Biggles, who was growling softly, his gaze darting between myself and Buddy. She began, her voice soft, "It's like he's guarding a precious bone, and he's afraid someone might take it away from him. And in this case, the bone is me?"

I couldn't help smiling at her analogy. "Exactly," I replied. "He sees you as his most prized possession, and he's willing to do whatever it takes to protect you, even if it means being aggressive towards others."

Mrs. Umber exhaled deeply, her shoulders drooped with realisation. "I always thought he was just being protective because he loved me. I never saw it as him trying to control the situation."

I leaned forward, ensuring I had her full attention. "Mrs. Umber, love and protection are closely linked. Sadly, when protection turns into aggression, it's not about love anymore. It's about dominance and control."

Pausing for a moment, I posed a question, "Imagine if a man behaved like Mr. Biggles, acting possessively, not allowing you speak or interact freely. What would you do if you had an overly jealous boyfriend acting this way?"

"I'd set him straight and let him know that behaviour isn't acceptable. I have a bit of a short fuse, myself." She blushed, clearly remembering how she threw that soup can at me.

"Exactly," I said, nodding. "And that's what we need to do with Mr. Biggles. You need to communicate that his behaviour is inappropriate. When you comforted him after he lunged at me, you were, in his eyes, supporting his actions. Instead of comforting, you should be correcting him, letting him know that such behaviour is not acceptable. It's similar to how you'd handle that hypothetical jealous boyfriend."

Her eyes widened, and she looked down at Mr. Biggles, who was now more subdued, though still eyeing me warily. "So, when I pulled him back and tried to soothe him, I was actually making things worse?"

I nodded, "Exactly, Mrs. Umber. By doing that, you were unintentionally reinforcing his belief that there was a threat. Our goal is to change that perception. We want Mr. Biggles to trust your judgement and understand that he doesn't need to be on high alert all the time."

"Please, call me Janice. I never realised how my reactions were influencing him. I thought I was just trying to protect others from him, but I see now that I was part of the problem.

"You know, I had another trainer before coming to you. She said she was a treat based trainer. She had a lot of qualifications and was quite expensive." she admitted, her voice tinged with frustration. "But she never explained it this way. All she did was use treats. She told me that eventually, Mr. Biggles would come to associate guests with treats and feeling good."

I raised an eyebrow, intrigued. "And how did that work out?"

Janice scoffed, "It didn't work. Every time someone came over, he'd get a treat, but he'd still growl and lunge, carrying on like a pork chop. And when I tried to reach out to the trainer for more guidance, she never responded. I felt so lost and frustrated."

"Did she offer anything else? Any other insights?" I asked, curiously.

"She did teach me about a clicker, but I never bothered with it because it was so irksome. She also told me that her information was backed by research and that I should not ever correct Mr. Biggles or tell him no. I should just ignore his behaviour like when he tries to bite people and reward him when he stops as this supposedly teaches him that not biting people gets rewarded."

"And how did that work out?" I asked.

Janice looked down at Mr. Biggles as he stared daggers at me. "It worked great, obviously," as she rolled her eyes.

I sighed sympathetically. "I'm sorry you had to go through that. Treats can be a useful tool in training, yet they're not a one-size-fits-all solution – especially in cases like Mr. Biggles', where the root of the problem is deeper than just wanting a treat."

Janice looked at me, her eyes filled with gratitude. "Thank you, Emily. I'm just glad I found you. The other trainer told me that if Mr. Biggles did not respond to the treat training method, that I should consider euthanising him. I understand, he can be quite vexing to other people, but he is very sweet and endearing to me. I refuse to accept that he should be euthanised."

Mr. Biggles continued eyeing me like he was going to use the Force to choke me out, I smiled warmly. "Great. Then let's fix this. We'll begin with the Leadership Walk.

"The Leadership Walk is more than just a simple walk, it's a dance, a conversation between you and Mr. Biggles. It's where you set the tone, establish boundaries, and communicate your expectations."

THE INSECURE JEALOUS BOYFRIEND

Janice looked at me curiously, "But we walk all the time."

I nodded, "Yes, however, a Leadership Walk is not a simple means of exercising or going someplace, it's a deep connection between you and your dog. When you're on a Leadership Walk, you're not just guiding Mr. Biggles' movements, you're also guiding his mind. You're teaching him to focus on you, to follow your lead, and to trust your decisions."

I paused, allowing the words sink in before continuing, "Right now, Mr. Biggles sees himself as the protector, the leader. He thinks he needs to guard you from every potential threat. Through the Leadership Walk, we can shift that dynamic. We can show him that you're the one in charge, that he can relax and trust you to make the decisions."

Janice seemed to ponder over this for a moment. "So, you're saying that by changing the way we walk, I can change our relationship?"

"Exactly," I began, my gaze shifting between Janice and Mr. Biggles. "The Leadership Walk isn't just about physical movement. It's a powerful tool that reestablishes leadership and clearly defines the nature of your relationship with Mr. Biggles. When executed with consistency and precision, it can reshape his perception of both you and his surroundings."

Janice's eyes followed Mr. Biggles, who had settled down, his gaze still locked onto me. "I never truly grasped the significance of a mere walk," she admitted, a hint of wonder in her voice.

I offered a reassuring smile. "Sometimes, it's the simplest actions that bring about the most profound changes. With dedication and patience, I'm confident that you and Mr. Biggles can forge a healthier bond."

You can also get videos of how to do the leadership walks and step by step instructions directly from George at www.DogLeadershipAcademy.com.

Without further ado, I gently took the leash from Janice's hand, passed a slip lead over his head, unclipped the leash from his harness, and initiated our Leadership Walk. Mr. Biggles was initially resistant, tugging and attempting to dictate our path. He was, however, not able to slip out as he would have on a regular collar or a harness. With each subtle correction and guidance, he gradually began to grasp the expectations set for him.

As we continued, I could feel the tension in Mr. Biggles' body start to dissipate. His previously rigid posture began to relax, and his focus shifted from the surroundings to me. The once aggressive and reactive chihuahua was now walking beside me, his pace matching mine.

Feeling confident in the progress we'd made, I decided to test Mr. Biggles further. Leading him towards the main street, we were soon surrounded by the hustle and bustle of pedestrians. Children laughing, people chatting, and the occasional cyclist whizzing by. Situations that would have previously sent Mr. Biggles into a frenzy. To my delight, and Janice's astonishment, Mr. Biggles remained calm. He walked beside me, his attention on me, completely ignoring the distractions around him. No lunging, no growling, just a calm and focused demeanour.

As we circled back to where Janice was waiting, her face was a picture of shock and awe. "I can't believe it," she whispered, her eyes wide with disbelief. "He's never been this calm around strangers before."

I handed the lead back to Janice, and gave Mr. Biggles gentle pats and praise. "It's all about communication and trust," I explained. "Once he understood what was expected of him and felt secure in his role, everything else fell into place. Now, let's teach you how to lead Mr. Biggles."

After an hour of practice, Janice was well on her way. We spoke of her next steps, and I extracted a promise that she'd continue to send me videos of their progress and ask any questions that may occur. As Buddy and I headed to the car, she gave me a hug. "Thank you, Emily. I never thought I'd see the day where Mr. Biggles could walk calmly among strangers. You truly have a gift."

~~~

Two weeks after that transformative day with Mr. Biggles, I was greeted by an unexpected delivery at my doorstep. A beautiful bouquet of flowers, their vibrant colours immediately brightening my living room. Nestled among the blooms was a photo. I couldn't help but chuckle as I looked at it. There was Mr. Biggles, his eyes glaring directly at the camera, that signature look of princely aloofness and disdain still evident. The truly heartwarming aspect was the backdrop. Mr. Biggles was surrounded by a group of young children, all beaming with joy and petting the chihuahua who was dressed in a rather motley assortment of doll clothes. While it wasn't his best look, he was handling it with the grace of a martyr.

A letter from Janice was enclosed. As I read Janice's words, a lump formed in my throat. "Dear Emily. Thanks to you, Mr. Biggles no longer bites people and knows his place in the world. You are truly a gift and a compassionate human being. Your mother must be so proud of you. The grandkids absolutely adore Mr. Biggles, now. I owe it all to you. Love, Janice."

Touched by her heartfelt words, I felt a surge of pride and satisfaction. Janice's kindness didn't end there. Along with the bouquet was a gift certificate to the Soupa Food, a local restaurant renowned for its extensive and delectable soup menu. I grinned.

Reading Mrs. Umber's note, my heart swelled with a mix of emotions. The words about my mother struck a deep chord within me, and I felt a familiar sting in my eyes. Tears welled, not just from the gratitude expressed in the note, also from the bittersweet memories of my mother. I could almost hear her voice, feel her comforting presence, and imagine her proud smile.

Every achievement, every milestone I reached, I wished she could witness. The mention of her in the note was a poignant reminder of the void she left behind, yet also of the values and lessons she instilled in me. I took a deep breath, trying to steady my emotions. Mrs. Umber's words were a testament to the impact we can have on others, even in the most unexpected ways. The thought that she believed my mother would be proud of me was both comforting and motivating.

I clutched the photo close to my heart for a moment, silently thanking Mrs. Umber for her kind words and my mother for her everlasting influence. The journey with Mr. Biggles and the subsequent gratitude from his owner was not just a professional achievement, it was a personal affirmation that I was on the right path, a path my mother would have been proud of.

Chapter Summary

In this chapter, readers are introduced to a common behavioural issue in dogs, humorously termed as the "Insecure Jealous Boyfriend Syndrome." This syndrome is characterised by a dog's overprotective nature, where they guard their owner as if they were a precious bone, preventing others from getting too close.

Key Points:

1. Defining the **Nature of the Relationship**: It's crucial for dog owners to establish the correct dynamics in their relationship with their pets. Dogs should understand that they are akin to children in the relationship, not the protectors or leaders.
2. **Correction and Reward**: When a dog begins to fixate or "lock on" to other people or potential threats, it's essential to correct this behaviour immediately. Owners should instruct their dog to cease the behaviour, often with a firm "knock it off" or a similar command. Once the dog complies reward them with a compliance marker, such as saying "Yes!" reinforces positive behaviour.
3. **The Power of the Leadership Walk**: One of the most effective tools in establishing the right relationship dynamics is the Leadership Walk. This activity is not just about physical exercise but is a means to communicate, establish and condition leadership and expectations to the dog.
4. **Leading the Walk**: During the Leadership Walk, the owner should always lead, ensuring the dog walks beside or behind them. Allowing a dog to lead the walk can reinforce the wrong dynamics, making the dog feel like they are in charge.
5. **Loose Leash Walking**: Make sure the leash is loose and not taut when encountering new people as this may trigger the dog into the need to be defensive.

By understanding and implementing these principles, dog owners can address and correct the "Insecure Jealous Boyfriend Syndrome," fostering a healthier, more balanced relationship with their pets.

For more information about George's leadership based training method, and get step by step video guide to human aggressive behaviour, come to www.DogLeadershipAcademy.com or scan the QRCode below.

We also have a specific guide book that addresses human aggressive behaviour available at all major book retailers. Look for "The Leadership Guide to Human Aggressive Behaviour".

24

The Kindness Paradox

The pavilion shaded me from the noon sun, a large banner reading "Free Class for Foster Carers" fluttered above, its message a testament to the promise I'd made to George and, more importantly, to myself, to pay it forward. The rigorous days under George's watchful eye, the countless homes I'd transformed over the past months, had led me to this lovely park in the city with flyers and business cards, helping people who foster dogs.

The local rescue had organised the event, and the turnout was more than I'd expected. Families, each with their own stories and struggles, gathered around, their rescued dogs of all shapes and sizes by their side. The air was thick with a mix of hope, desperation, and the unmistakable bond between human and dog.

I stepped confidently into the training area, Buddy trotting beside me. "Ladies and gentlemen," I began, "meet Buddy. He was once in a pound, on the brink of euthanasia. He was classified as dog aggressive. And now, look at him." With a subtle gesture, I signalled Buddy to walk beside me, heel without a leash, and without the lure of treats. As we moved in harmony, I softly whispered a command and stomped my foot. Instantly, Buddy sat, remaining still and attentive as I continued my presentation.

Moments passed and, with a simple release command, Buddy returned to a perfect heel position by my side. The crowd erupted in applause, not just for Buddy's impeccable behaviour, also for the journey he had undertaken—from a bleak beginning to this moment of triumph.

"This," I declared, "is the power of leadership-based training. It's not about bribing with treats, but about building a bond of trust and understanding. It's about guiding our dogs with clarity and consistency."

The sun's rays filtered through the trees, casting dappled shadows on the ground. As Buddy and I stood in the park, surrounded by eager foster families. Each family had a story, each dog a past, and they looked to me for guidance. One by one, Buddy and I had been counselling, advising, and making appointments for personalised sessions.

A couple approached, their faces etched with concern. Clinging to the woman's leg was a border collie, its body language screaming fear. The man began, "We just got Luna from the pound recently. We've tried everything - treats, coaxing, showering her with love. But she's just so... shut down."

I knelt down, keeping a respectful distance from the collie, and looked into its eyes. They were pools of fear and uncertainty. Rising, I turned to the couple. "I know it's hard," I began gently, "but sometimes, the best thing to do is nothing."

The woman looked at me, confusion evident in her eyes. "But we want to help Luna," she protested.

I nodded, understanding her desperation. "I know. But right now, she's overwhelmed. She needs space. Let her come to you when she's ready." I paused then continued, "Have you heard of Counter-conditioning?"

The couple exchanged glances, then shook their heads. I took a deep breath, preparing to impart one of the most crucial lessons in dog training.

"Counter-conditioning is about changing a dog's emotional response to something they find scary. For instance, if Luna is afraid of people, you can pair the presence of people with something she loves, like treats or toys. Over time, she'll start associating people with positive things. Here is how to practice Counter-conditioning.

"1. Start Slowly: Begin by simply being in the same room as Luna without directly interacting with her. Over time, she'll start to see that your presence isn't threatening.

"2. Positive Associations: Instead of directly giving Luna treats, place a treat near you and let her approach and take it (if she is comfortable to eat), otherwise, throw the treats close to her for her to take the treat without the fear of being touched by you. This will help her associate coming to you with positive rewards.

"3. Gradual Exposure: Once Luna is comfortable taking treats near you, introduce her to one new person at a time in a controlled environment. That person should avoid direct eye contact and let Luna approach them.

"4. Consistency: Repeat these sessions regularly, ensuring that each interaction is positive and stress-free for Luna."

The couple listened intently, hanging on to every word. "However," I added, "it's essential to start slow. Don't force interactions. Let her observe you from a distance, and reward her for calm behaviour. Gradually decrease the distance as she becomes more comfortable. It always has to be on her terms. Never force intimacy. If anything, just ignore her for the next few days. Let her come to you. Here's my card. Please stay in touch with me, call me any time and we can work together to bring her out of her shell."

Another family, the Harrisons, stepped forward. They held a leash attached to a robust Amstaff named Boss. Mrs. Harrison, her voice shaking, explained their ordeal. "He guards. He's not just guarding his food, he even guards random things. We've tried everything our previous trainer taught us, including the 'Yes' compliance marker and Counter-conditioning, but nothing seems to work."

Mr. Harrison added, "Our trainer said that if he doesn't respond to treats and praises, he's untrainable. She even suggested euthanasia." He paused, taking a deep breath, "We even mentioned possibly seeking help from George, but she was horrified. She warned us against anyone who isn't a treat based trainer, claiming they use threats and stress the dog out."

I felt a pang of sadness and frustration. Taking a moment to gather my thoughts, I responded, "It's disheartening to hear that a trainer would rather recommend euthanasia than consider alternative training methods. While positive reinforcement is essential, it's not the only tool in the toolbox. Every dog is unique, and what works for one might not work for another."

I looked them squarely in the eyes, "Your previous trainer's stance is a classic example of the Kindness Paradox. In trying to be kind and avoid any perceived stress for the dog, she's recommending the most extreme method, which isn't really working for Boss."

The Harrisons nodded. I continued, "Let's work together to find a balanced approach that suits Boss' needs. There's always hope, and with patience and the right techniques, we can help him overcome his guarding tendencies.

"First, let's understand where resource guarding comes from. It's typically a learned behaviour or success strategy at a formative moment in the dog's life. Imagine a young puppy, like Boss, never having enough food, being bullied, and having his food stolen by others in the litter. In such situations, they develop a coping mechanism. To survive, they feel the need to fight for everything. It's a scarcity mentality."

The Harrisons exchanged glances. "So, he's acting out of fear of not having enough?" Mrs. Harrison asked.

"Exactly," I replied. "Our goal is to transition Boss from this scarcity mindset to an abundance mentality. We want him to understand that there's more than enough and that he doesn't need to guard resources aggressively."

I motioned for them to bring Boss closer. "We'll start with the Leave It command. This will teach Boss to willingly give up what he's guarding. Let's try a little exercise, shall we? When I say "Leave It," please give his leash a little snap. Our goal is to gain his attention back to us and away from the resource he wants to guard."

I reached into my duffle bag and pulled out a bowl and some kibble. Placing the bowl next to me and I patiently waited for Boss' attention to be drawn to it. As he made a move to dive into the bowl, I asserted, "Leave It." Mr. Harrison snapped the lead to coincide with my command. When he refrained from eating, I enthusiastically exclaimed "Yes!" and promptly handed him a piece of rotisserie chicken from a bag I had been keeping in my pocket.

After Boss enjoyed the piece of chicken, I then allowed him access to the bowl of food, ensuring he understood that he hadn't lost out on his meal, rather, he had gained an extra treat by listening. His tail wagged in contentment and gratitude for the nice snack.

Turning to the Harrisons, I elaborated, "The principle here is called 'Trading

Up.' Our goal is to teach Boss that by momentarily holding back and following instruction, not only does he receive an additional reward, but he also gets to enjoy his original food. He loses nothing and gains more by learning Leave It."

Mr. Harrison summarised, "So, it's about teaching him the value of patience and that there's always more abundance awaiting him."

Mrs. Harrison then interjected, "But what about when he guards our shoes or the TV remote control? It's not just food he's possessive over."

I nodded, understanding the depth of their predicament. "For items like shoes and remotes, continue practising the 'Leave It' command. The principle remains the same. When Boss leaves the item he's guarding upon your command, mark that behaviour with 'Yes!' and reward him with something he values more. Over time, he'll understand that by giving up what he's guarding, he gets something even better in return. And importantly, he'll also realise that no one is taking the original item away from him. It's still there for him.

"Dogs often value things based on our reactions to them. If he perceives that you desperately want the item, it increases its value in his eyes. By showing him that you're not interested in taking it away permanently, its value diminishes.

"For safety during these exercises," I continued, "I'd recommend keeping Boss on a martingale collar attached to a leash or a slip lead. The design of the martingale ensures it won't slip off his head, providing an added layer of security."

Mrs. Harrison scribbled down some notes on the back of a flyer I handed her. "Thank you, Emily. We'll give these techniques a go. But what if we run into issues or need more hands-on help?"

I offered a comforting smile, "Always remember, you can call me anytime if you need guidance with Boss. I'm here to help. My phone and email are right here on the front of the flyer."

I then addressed the crowd, "For those of you out there looking for more personalised assistance, especially with challenging dog behaviours, I highly recommend checking out George's website at http://www.DogLeadershipA

cademy.com. Not only will you find step-by-step video tutorials, you'll also find the chance for personalised interaction with George's leadership teaching methods and being able to ask questions and receive detailed answers."

The Harrisons exchanged grateful glances. "Thank you, Emily," Mr. Harrison said. "We're hopeful now. We'll do everything we can to ensure Boss feels secure and loved in our home. Is there anything else we should be doing, concurrently?"

"Yes, you'll benefit greatly by establishing a clear leadership hierarchy. Boss needs to see you as his leaders, not merely the nice people that feed him. One of the best ways to do that is through Leadership Walks. A Leadership Walk is not just about physical exercise. A Leadership Walk sets up a working relationship between you and Boss. It reinforces the idea that you lead, and he follows. Over time, this consistent leadership on walks will translate to respect and trust at home."

After demonstrating a Leadership Walk with Buddy, Mrs. Harrison asked, "But hasn't pack theory been debunked? I've read articles that say it's outdated and not applicable to domestic dogs."

I smiled gently and sighed, "Ah, the age-old debate on pack theory." I began, "While it's true that dogs have been domesticated for thousands of years, they still share many behavioural characteristics with their wild ancestors, the wolves. The original researcher, David Mech, did propose an 'alpha wolf' theory, then he later clarified his stance."

I continued, "Mech explained that wolves, and by extension dogs, form a family structure with one or more leaders in the pack, much like any human family unit. It's not about dominance in a negative sense, but rather about guidance, leadership, and setting boundaries."

Mrs. Harrison raised an eyebrow, intrigued. "So, you're saying the whole 'alpha' concept was misunderstood?"

I nodded, "Exactly. Many treat based trainers, unfortunately, took Mech's initial theory out of context to further their agenda. Mech himself has tried to rectify this misconception of his work through multiple papers and clarifications. His original theory has been, for lack of a better term, butchered by many trainers who are driven by a certain narrative and agenda."

Mrs. Harrison looked a bit overwhelmed, "It's so hard to know what to believe with so much conflicting information out there."

I reached out, placing a reassuring hand on her arm. "I understand your confusion, Mrs. Harrison. The world of dog training is filled with various schools of thought. At the end of the day, it's about finding a balanced approach that works for both the dog and the owner. And always remember, every dog is unique. What works for one might not work for another."

She smiled, gratitude evident in her eyes. "Thank you, Emily. It's comforting to know there are people like you who genuinely care about helping dogs and their families navigate these challenges."

"Thank you. I truly love my work. It's the most gratifying job I've ever held. Just remember, with dedication and consistency, I believe Boss will turn over a new leaf. It's all about timely clear communication, understanding, and mutual respect."

As the day came to a close, the demonstrators were abuzz with the residual excitement of the event. Attendees exchanged stories and insights, their conversations filled with enthusiasm. As I was packing up, I took a moment to bend down and nuzzle my face into Buddy, planting a gentle kiss on his forehead. He responded with affectionate licks, his tail wagged with contentment.

Out of the corner of my eye, I noticed Francis, the event organiser, standing nearby, her posture suggesting she wanted a word with me. As I straightened up, Buddy, sensing he was free to mingle, trotted over to Francis. His tail wagged even faster, and he leaned into her, offering his paw in a friendly gesture.

"Emily, I just wanted to express my gratitude. Your session today was truly enlightening, and it's evident how much passion and knowledge you bring to the world of dog training."

"Thank you," I beamed.

Francis continued, "The rise of treat-based training has led to an alarming increase in the number of dogs being surrendered due to behavioural issues. It's heartbreaking. Dogs, much like children, need to understand boundaries. They need to know right from wrong, and sometimes, that requires correction. In the wild, they correct each other—it's a natural part of their social structure."

"I've seen it too," I admitted. "Dogs become confused about their roles in the household because their owners are afraid to set boundaries. It's like the trend in parenting where parents don't want to tell their children 'no' or discipline them, resulting in more misbehaving kids. Similarly, when things get out of hand with their dogs, families are quick to give up and surrender them."

She sighed, "Exactly. And these treat-based trainers? They cherry-pick the science that aligns with their narrative, not necessarily what's best for the dog and the humans. It's frustrating to see so many dogs suffer because of it."

We stood in silence for a moment, both lost in our thoughts. I felt a renewed sense of purpose, grateful for the validation and the reminder of why I had chosen this path. "Thank you, it's reassuring to know that there are others who share the same beliefs and are working toward the same goal."

She smiled, "Keep doing what you're doing, Emily. The dogs need voices like yours."

I took a moment to reflect on the day's events. Each family, each dog, had a unique story, a unique challenge, yet they all shared a common thread; the desire for a harmonious relationship. By guiding these foster families and their dogs, I was not just helping them in the present, I was setting the stage for these dogs to transition smoothly into their forever homes, ensuring they wouldn't face the heartbreak of being returned to the shelter or, worse, euthanized.

This is why I pour my heart and soul into what I do. Every life, every soul, matters. Every dog deserves a chance at a loving home, and every family deserves the joy of a well-behaved pet. My mission goes beyond just training; it's about saving lives, one dog at a time.

As the crowd began to disperse, I felt a renewed sense of purpose. By spreading awareness of leadership-based training methodologies and educating more people about our methods, we can change the narrative. We can ensure that fewer dogs are surrendered, fewer dogs face the bleak fate of euthanasia. Every session, every class, every interaction brings us one step closer to that dream. As I packed up my things and headed home, I carried with me the hope and determination to continue making a difference, one dog at a time.

Chapter Summary

This chapter delves into a paradoxical stance prevalent within the dog training industry. There exists a cohort of trainers who, while staunchly opposing the use of corrective tools or methods—deeming them inhumane— advocate for euthanasia in challenging behavioural cases. Such a perspective reveals a cognitive dissonance, where the adherence to certain ideological principles and the desire to occupy a moral high ground seem to overshadow genuine concern for the well-being of the dogs and their families. Tragically, this often leaves families in the heart-wrenching position of having to surrender or euthanize their pets.

Shut Down Dog Treatment Plan
  1. **Recognizing a Shut Down Dog**:
  - These dogs often display signs of extreme fear, avoidance, and may seem unresponsive to stimuli.
  2. **The Importance of Space**:
  - Avoid crowding or overwhelming the dog.
  - Give the dog ample space and allow it to have a safe zone where it can retreat and feel secure like a crate.
  3. **Let the Dog Initiate**:
  - Instead of forcing interactions, wait for the dog to approach you.
  - This allows the dog to control the pace of the interaction, reducing anxiety.
  4. **Counter Conditioning Principles**:
  - Aim to change the dog's emotional response to previously fearful stimuli.
  - Pair the presence of potentially scary situations or items with positive

rewards, such as treats or toys.

5. **Gradual Exposure**:

- Slowly introduce the dog to new environments, people, or other stimuli.

- Start with short, neutral or positive sessions and gradually increase the duration and complexity as the dog becomes more comfortable.

6. **Patience is Key**:

- Understand that progress may be slow, and setbacks can occur. You are dealing with a dog that may have experienced trauma or had very unfortunate history with humans. It takes time and patience for the dog to learn to trust.

- Celebrate small victories and remain consistent in your approach.

By applying these principles with patience and understanding, a shut down dog can gradually learn to trust and engage with its environment positively.

Counter Conditioning for a Fearful, Shut Down Dog

To change the dog's negative emotional response to a particular stimulus by associating it with positive outcomes.

1. Identify the Trigger:

- Determine what specific stimuli or situations cause fear or anxiety in the dog. This could be a person, another animal, a particular sound, etc.

2. Start at a Distance:

- Begin the training sessions at a distance where the dog notices the stimulus but does not show signs of fear or anxiety.

3. Pair the Trigger with Positive Reinforcements:

- As soon as the dog notices the trigger, offer a high-value treat or favourite toy. The goal is for the dog to associate the trigger with positive outcomes.

4. Gradually Decrease the Distance:

- Over multiple sessions, slowly decrease the distance between the dog and the trigger, always ensuring the dog remains below its fear threshold.

- Continue to offer treats or toys each time the dog notices the trigger without reacting negatively.

5. Monitor the Dog's Body Language:

- Look for signs of relaxation or curiosity towards the trigger. This indicates that the counter-conditioning is working.

- If the dog shows signs of stress or fear, increase the distance and go back to a previous step where the dog was comfortable.

6. Increase the Difficulty Gradually:

- Once the dog is comfortable at a closer distance, introduce mild variations of the trigger (e.g., if the dog is afraid of people, have a person stand up instead of sitting).

- Always reward positive or neutral reactions to the trigger.

7. Practice Regularly:

- Consistency is key. Hold short, regular sessions rather than infrequent, longer ones.

- The more positive associations the dog has with the trigger, the quicker the progress.

8. Seek Professional Help if Needed:

- If the dog's fear is deeply ingrained or if you're unsure about the process, consider seeking the help of a professional dog behaviourist or trainer experienced in counter-conditioning. For more personalised help with any training problem come to http://www.DogLeadershipAcademy.com.

9. Celebrate Small Victories:

- Every positive interaction the dog has with the trigger is a step forward. Celebrate these moments and be patient, understanding that progress might be slow.

10. Maintain the Progress:

- Once the dog is consistently showing positive or neutral reactions to the trigger, continue to expose them to it occasionally, reinforcing with treats or praise, to maintain their positive associations.

Remember, the goal of counter-conditioning is to change the dog's emotional response, so it's essential to ensure each interaction is positive and stress-free.

Resource Guarding Summary:
1. **Understanding Resource Guarding**:
- Originates from a scarcity mindset, often developed during puppyhood due to competition for resources.
- Transitioning a dog from this scarcity mindset to an abundance mentality is crucial.

2. **The "Leave It" Command**:
- Train the dog to momentarily hold back from what they're guarding.
- Mark the desired behaviour with a "YES!" and reward with something of higher value.
- The dog learns that by holding back, they gain more, reinforcing the abundance mentality. Teaching them the concept of "trading up" rather than losing out.

3. **Value Perception**:
- Dogs often assign value to items based on our reactions.
- Showing disinterest in an item can diminish its value in the dog's eyes.

4. **Safety First**:
- Use a martingale collar and leash or a slip lead during training exercises to ensure everyone's safety. This ensures that the dog doesn't slip off and become out of control.

5. **Establishing Leadership**:
- Leadership Walks are essential, not just for exercise but to establish a clear leadership hierarchy.
- Consistent leadership during walks translates to respect and trust at home.

6. **Seeking Expertise**:
- In complex situations, especially like resource guarding, it's beneficial to work directly with a dog behaviourist.

Our mission is to spread awareness of leadership based training methodology as an alternative to the mainstream treat based training narrative. For more information about our mission, come to www.DogLeadershipAcademy.com.

25

The Behaviourist

Months later.

I sat on Andrew's balcony, a cup of tea in hand, basking in the warmth of the afternoon sun. The soft chirping of the birds and the distant noise of the city provided a gentle backdrop to my thoughts.

It was incredible to think about how much had changed in the past year. From the monotonous grind of managing a store, where I felt like a cog in a machine, to where every day was filled with purpose and passion. My heart swelled with pride as I thought about the dogs I had helped, the families I had supported, and the difference I was making in the world. Each client wasn't just a paycheck; they were a life changed, a family made whole again, and a story of hope.

What had begun as me reaching out to save Buddy had, in fact, been Buddy saving me.

Buddy lay by my side, his head resting on my lap. I stroked his head, lost in thought. He had been the catalyst for all of this. If it hadn't been for him, I might still be stuck in that grocery store, feeling unfulfilled and yearning for more. He had brought so much joy and purpose into my life, and I was eternally grateful.

And then there was Andrew. He had been my rock throughout this journey. His unwavering support, his expertise, and his genuine care had been instrumental in my success. Together, we were a team, and I cherished every moment we spent together.

As I reflected on my journey, a thought nagged at me. I remembered the mysterious benefactor who had sponsored my training. I had never gotten the chance to thank them. Picking up my phone, I dialled Jan from Pound Jailbreakers.

"Jan! It's Emily. I was just reflecting on everything and wanted to reach out and thank you. And I was hoping to get in touch with the benefactor who sponsored my training."

There was a pause on the other end. "Emily," Jan began, her voice filled with confusion, "I thought you knew. The benefactor never came through with the funds."

I was taken aback. "What do you mean?"

Jan explained, "We never received any money from them. I assumed you had found another way to cover the costs."

My mind raced, trying to piece together the puzzle.

I sat on the couch, phone pressed to my ear, trying to process Jan's words. I was momentarily breathless.

After a brief chat, I ended the call. Andrew, returning from the kitchen with our teapot refilled, sat on the other side of me, Millie at his feet.

"Emily," he began, his voice gentle, "there's something you should know. I wasn't supposed to tell you this, yet I think you deserve to know the truth." He paused, searching my eyes for understanding. "Your benefactor… it was your mother."

The weight of his words hit me like a ton of bricks. My mother? The woman who had always put me first, who had sacrificed so much throughout her life? The woman who had raised me, cared for me, and loved me unconditionally, even though I wasn't her biological child… even though she had expressed concerns, she had been my benefactor… then it dawned on me, the cruise she cancelled… she must have used that money to fund my dream.

I looked at Andrew, unable to hide my tears. He held my hand and explained, "Your mum phoned George. They spoke at length. She had a lot of concerns about Buddy and his record, George's thoughts on your chances at success… She told him to give her a few days and she'd send the money to him."

"That money came from her retirement cruise to New Zealand. She was so looking forward to it." I sobbed as the raw emotion consumed me. The depth of her love, her unwavering belief in me, was humbling. She had silently been my pillar, supporting me even in her final days.

Andrew gently wiped away my tears. "She wanted you to focus on your training, on your future. She believed in you, Emily, just as we all do."

I took a deep breath, trying to find the words. "I never got to thank her," I whispered regretfully.

Even in my grief, the song "Don't Stop Believin'" looped through my mind. She had never stopped believing in me. She may not have said it in as many words, but she always showed it.

The love and sacrifice of my mother, combined with the unwavering support of those around me, filled me with a renewed sense of purpose. I was determined to honour her memory by being the best dog behaviourist I could be, and to continue making a difference in the lives of dogs and their owners.

As the evening shadows deepened, I felt such hope and such gratitude. My journey had been filled with challenges, yet it had also been filled with love, support, and unwavering belief. With that knowledge, I felt ready to face whatever the future held.

26

Epilogue

I wrote this book out of a compelling need to give a voice to the countless voiceless victims: the dogs who have been abandoned, surrendered, and ultimately euthanized. The world is filled with tales of dogs who have been misunderstood, mistreated, and given up on. But it's also filled with stories of redemption, love, and second chances.

The theme of this book could have taken many forms—it could have been a tribute to the countless dogs I've met and saved, or a showcase of the training methods I've developed. But at its heart, this book is about something deeper: hope and belief. It's about the hope for change, the resilience of the human spirit, and the unconditional love that our canine companions bring into our lives.

While I didn't ultimately name the book *Don't Stop Believing*, that message remains its underlying theme. It's more than just a song lyric or a mantra for personal growth—it's a call to action. It's a reminder to every dog owner, every pet lover, and anyone who has ever faced a challenge: Don't give up. Keep believing in the power of transformation and the possibility of a better tomorrow.

To you, your dog might be a part of your life. For that dog, you are their whole world. You are their protector, their provider, and their family. And while it's easy to get frustrated or feel overwhelmed, it's crucial to remember the bond that ties you together.

EPILOGUE

This book was written because I wanted to inspire you to not give up. Don't Stop Believing. Don't Stop Believing in yourself, your dreams, and ultimately, Don't Stop Believing in your dog. I wanted this book to also act as a guide to help you navigate the challenges of dog ownership. It's a testament to the transformative power of love, compassion, and understanding. It's a reminder that with the right tools and mindset, you can overcome any obstacle and forge a deeper, more meaningful connection with your furry friend.

So, as you turn the last pages, I hope you feel inspired. Inspired to look at your dog with fresh eyes, inspired to appreciate the little moments, inspired to cherish the bond you share, and, more than anything, I hope you feel empowered. Empowered to face challenges head-on, to seek out knowledge, and to be the best dog owner you can be.

Remember, every dog deserves a second chance, and every person has the power to make a difference. So, Don't Stop Believing in the potential for change, in the strength of your bond, and in the love that you and your dog share. In the end, that belief can move mountains.

If you have benefited from the knowledge in this book, are inspired by it, or know someone who has a dog with behaviour issues, please pay it forward. **Please share it with at least two friends.**

Your friend,

George Tran
Dog Behaviourist
Don't stop believing

27

Who Was Buddy?

WHO WAS BUDDY?

Buddy

BEYOND TREATS: REVOLUTIONARY DOG TRAINING FOR LASTING BEHAVIOUR CHANGE

Few people know that a pit bull named Buddy changed my life. I began my career early, creating an e-commerce company from my living room, programming the whole thing myself. It eventually became one of the largest e-commerce companies in the world, that I launched during the Dotcom boom. By 32, I had achieved what many only dream of—taking my company public and "retiring" young. I shifted into real estate investments, but everything collapsed with the 2008 Global Financial Crisis. My savings, properties—all gone. I was left feeling adrift, lost, and eventually spiraled into depression, spending entire days in bed, lacking motivation to do anything. I would play computer games all day and, at times, even felt suicidal, unable to find a reason to get up.

One day, while scrolling through a rescue site, I came across Buddy. A magnificent pit bull . Something about Buddy called to me. Despite knowing he was labeled "human-aggressive" with a difficult past, I felt an undeniable pull. I was told he was absolutely great with other dogs.

Without knowing why, I felt compelled to adopt him. I mean, who does that? Maybe God had a plan for me and Buddy. I don't know why I did it, honestly. I decided to take Buddy on as my mission—to be his advocate, protector, and trainer. If he was going to have a second chance, I would be everything he needed.

Buddy gave me a reason to get up every morning. Despite his spinal issues and clumsy gait, his spirit was unbroken. As months passed, Buddy's strength grew, and soon his walk looked almost normal. But our biggest challenge was his reactivity toward humans. Isolated in a backyard for most of his life, Buddy saw some people in public as a threat. He would lunge at random people who came too close to him. But I was all in—ready to commit to him for life if that's what it took.

I immersed myself in learning everything I could about dog training. He needed me to be his unwavering guide, his protector, his daddy.

Buddy wasn't just a dog I rescued—he was my therapy dog before therapy dogs were even a thing. He gave me purpose, discipline, and, above all, joy. He was my constant companion, keeping me grounded through every high and low.

From Saving Buddy to Saving More Dogs

Buddy taught me more than any book or business venture ever could. Without realizing it, I'd discovered my talent for training dogs, especially the "hard cases" like Buddy. When Buddy passed away from a heart attack, without going into detail, it inspired me to do more. I began fostering other dogs with behavioural issues, and I realized I had a gift for helping those out of options. My unique approach, built on structure rather than treats, worked especially well with these challenging dogs. Rescue organizations began reaching out, and I took on some of the most aggressive and "hopeless" cases. I have honestly lost count of how many dogs I have saved privately.

Word spread, and more people began asking for my help. What started as a personal mission to save Buddy became a calling, and I found myself becoming a dog behaviourist, helping hundreds of dogs and their owners build stronger, healthier relationships.

Buddy not only saved me, but in the end, he set me on this path. Now, with this book, I hope his legacy lives on—in every dog we save and every life we change.

Please. **Help me save more dogs**. <u>Please tell others about Buddy and me</u>. Write a review on your favourite online bookstore like Amazon. Let's start a movement and be part of the awakening to a more effective method of training dogs and saving lives.

Your friend,

BEYOND TREATS: REVOLUTIONARY DOG TRAINING FOR LASTING BEHAVIOUR CHANGE

George Tran
Dog Behaviourist

28

Additional Resources

While this book provides a solid foundation for understanding dog behaviour, we encourage you to explore further resources that can help you on your journey. At www.dogleadershipacademy.com, you'll find a wealth of additional support and tools, all designed to make training your dog easier and more effective.

Here's what you'll find:

- **Personalized Advice**: Ask our system for specific advice on any behaviour issue you're facing and receive detailed step by step answers to your questions.
- **Knowledge Base**: Access our comprehensive knowledge base filled with detailed instructions on various training techniques.
- **Step by Step training videos**: Let us show you how to deal with each behaviour or technique such as bracing, loose leash walking or the leadership walk through our video tutorials.
- **Hundreds of Hours of Training Content**: George has spent countless hours refining his methods and offering step-by-step guides to address a wide range of dog behaviour challenges.
- **24/7 Access**: All resources are available anytime, free of charge. No credit card required—just helpful, straightforward information to guide

you.

Unlock the Full Potential of Your Dog Training Journey

Ready to take the principles of *Beyond Treats* to the next level? Download the **FREE Beyond Treats Companion Workbook** at www.dogleadershipacademy.com and gain access to the tools you need to transform your relationship with your dog!

This workbook is the step-by-step guide to help you implement the leadership-based training methods from Beyond Treats. It's packed with actionable strategies, daily plans, and tracking tools to set you and your dog up for success.

The Beyond Treats Companion Workbook provides you with:

- **Practical Exercises**
- Learn exactly how to perform leadership walks, marker training, and impulse control exercises.
- **Daily Action Plans**
- Structured day-by-day tasks to help you stay consistent and on track.
- **Checklists for Success**
- Ensure you cover all key training steps with easy-to-follow daily checklists.
- **Progress Trackers**
- Measure your improvement and see how far you and your dog have come.
- **Step-by-Step Guidance**
- Clear instructions that simplify complex concepts into achievable daily actions.
- **Self Assessment Insights**

ADDITIONAL RESOURCES

- Tips to help you build respect, reinforce boundaries, and foster a harmonious relationship.

Don't miss this opportunity to make lasting changes in your dog's behavior and your relationship. Visit www.dogleadershipacademy.com now to download your free copy of the *Beyond Treats Companion Workbook*.

Your journey toward a respectful, harmonious relationship with your dog begins here. Let's get started!

Take Your Dog Training Knowledge to the Next Level

If you loved the insights and stories in *Beyond Treats* but crave a more structured, in-depth approach, the **Dog Leadership Training Guide** is exactly what you need.

Where *Beyond Treats* introduces leadership-based dog training through relatable, story-driven examples, the **Dog Leadership Training Guide** presents the same principles in a traditional manual format. With additional deep dives and expanded insights, this guide offers a comprehensive understanding of the framework behind earning your dog's trust and respect.
Best of all. It's FREE.

Why Get the Dog Leadership Training Guide?

- **Expanded Insights:**
- Go beyond the basics with a deeper exploration of leadership and respect-based training.
- **Traditional Format:**
- A structured manual for those who prefer clear, step-by-step explanations over storytelling.
- **Deep Dive Into Leadership Principles:**
- Uncover the psychology behind your dog's behavior and how to trans-

form your relationship through effective leadership.
- **Earn Lasting Respect:**
- Learn how to cultivate a relationship where your dog follows your lead because they trust and respect you—not because you have treats.
- **Practical and Comprehensive:**
- Clear, concise breakdowns of the key methods to help you understand *why* they work, not just *how* to do them.

What You'll Gain

- A greater understanding of the science behind leadership-based training.
- Actionable strategies to address problem behaviors and build a harmonious relationship.
- Clarity on why love and respect are not the same—and how to achieve both with your dog.
- Confidence in your role as a calm, competent leader your dog trusts.

Don't Miss Out

Whether you're new to dog training or want to deepen your knowledge, the **Dog Leadership Training Guide** is the perfect companion to *Beyond Treats*.

Gain a comprehensive understanding of how to lead with compassion, structure, and authority. Start your journey toward a more respectful, cooperative, and fulfilling relationship with your dog today.

Visit **www.dogleadershipacademy.com** to download your **free copy** now!

You can also buy a print version from Amazon and other leading online retailers. Just search for "Dog Leadership Training Guide"

29

Help Me Save More Dogs

My mission is to end the suffering of dogs due to misunderstanding, ineffective and outdated training methods. Too many dogs end up surrendered or euthanized simply because they weren't given the chance to thrive through effective leadership-based training. But I can't do this alone, and I need your help to spread the word.

If more people understood the importance of **leadership based training**, we could reduce the number of dogs being given up or put down. Please share what you've learned with friends and family, and help spread awareness about **leadership based training**. It makes a real difference for both dogs and their owners. Forward a copy of this book or tell every dog owner you know—together, we can ensure more dogs get the chance they deserve.

To spread awareness, please post about what you learned from "Beyond Treats" on Facebook, and other social media platforms. Recommend the book on dog training groups and forums. Use the **hashtag #beyondtreats**.

It would also mean the world to me if you could **leave a review of my book on Amazon**. Share just one "aha!" moment you have learned. Reviews help people make informed decisions, and your thoughts can help spread awareness even further. If you've found value in what I've shared, please leave your review here:

https://amzn.to/3NHxoK3

BEYOND TREATS: REVOLUTIONARY DOG TRAINING FOR LASTING BEHAVIOUR CHANGE

Scan to leave Review

Thank you for your support. Together, we can make a real difference in the lives of countless dogs.

30

Also By George Tran

Specific Behaviour Guides

George will be releasing additional guidebooks that focuses on solving specific dog behaviour issues. These guides provide you with **detailed step by step instructions** that are specific to your dog's behaviour issues using a leadership based framework. Look for "The Leadership Guide Series" at your favourite online book retailer.

Some of our titles include:
  The Beyond Treats Companion Workbook
  The Dog Leadership Training Guide
  The Dog Leadership Guide to Anxiety/Fearful Behaviour
  The Dog Leadership Guide to Toilet Training
  The Dog Leadership Guide to Leash Pulling
  The Dog Leadership Guide to Jumping on People
  The Dog Leadership Guide to Separation Anxiety and Excessive Barking
  The Dog Leadership Guide to Dog Reactivity
  The Dog Leadership Guide to Human Aggression
  And much more...

Whether you're struggling with a specific issue or want to deepen your understanding of dog behaviour, these resources will give you the tools and knowledge to succeed.

Look for these books at your favourite online book retailer such as Amazon, Google, Apple, etc. Or come to www.dogleadershipacademy.com.

31

Backed by Science

For those wondering whether a leadership-based methodology in dog training aligns with **scientific consensus** and is supported by empirical evidence rather than anecdotal evidence, the answer is a definitive yes. This chapter will delve into the research that **validates leadership-based training as an effective, humane, and scientifically grounded approach**. Far from relying on outdated notions or guesswork, this method reflects principles firmly established in psychology, animal behaviour, and cognitive science, solidifying its place within the scientific consensus.

The Core of Leadership-Based Training

Leadership-based training involves providing dogs with clear guidance, consistent rules, and responsive interactions. This approach recognizes that dogs, like humans, benefit from structure and feedback to navigate their environment successfully. By combining high expectations with emotional responsiveness, leadership-based training mirrors the well-researched authoritative parenting style observed in human psychology. This balance promotes emotional security, cognitive development, and cooperative behaviour.

Scientific Foundations of Leadership-Based Training

1. Increased Responsiveness Through Structure and Guidance
Van Herwijnen et al. (2018):

Published in PLOS ONE in 2018 *"Animal Cognition"*, this study explored how different dog-directed parenting styles influence behaviour. The researchers identified three primary styles: authoritarian-correction, authoritative-training, and authoritative-intrinsic value.

- **Key Findings:**
- The authoritative-training style, characterized by firm guidance combined with high responsiveness, was associated with effective leash handling and greater owner-directed attention. Dogs trained under this method demonstrated improved communication with their owners and heightened attentiveness.
- **Conclusion:**
- Structured, responsive leadership helps dogs focus on their owners, reducing confusion and fostering cooperation.

2. Emotional Security Through Authoritative Interaction
Brubaker and Udell (2022):

Researchers from Oregon State University conducted the study "Does Pet Parenting Style predict the social and problem-solving behaviour of pet dogs (Canis lupus familiaris)?" published in *Animal Cognition*. This study evaluated the influence of various parenting styles on the development of attachment security and problem-solving abilities in dogs.

- **Key Findings:**
- Dogs with authoritative owners—defined by clear expectations paired with emotional responsiveness—exhibited secure attachments, increased persistence in problem-solving tasks, and better responsiveness to social cues.
- **Conclusion:**

- Leadership-based training enhances emotional security in dogs, allowing them to engage more effectively with their environment and handlers.

3. Improved behaviour and Well-Being
Wendy Lyons Sunshine (2023):

In an article published in *Psychology Today*, Sunshine explored how parenting styles translate to dog training. She compared neglectful, permissive, authoritarian, and authoritative approaches.

- **Key Findings:**
- The authoritative style, which blends clear expectations with positive reinforcement, was consistently associated with better outcomes in dog behaviour, emotional stability, and overall well-being.
- **Conclusion:**
- This approach avoids the pitfalls of permissiveness (confusion and instability) and authoritarianism (fear and stress), providing a balanced and scientifically supported methodology.

Why Leadership-Based Training Works

Leadership-based training seamlessly integrates positive reinforcement with additional components of operant conditioning, counter-conditioning, and a parenting framework. This approach combines the best of both worlds: the science-backed effectiveness of positive reinforcement and the essential leadership guidance that both people and animals instinctively seek, especially in high-stress situations.

In such moments, while treat-based, all-positive methods effectively create positive associations, they often lack the directive leadership dogs require to navigate crises. Just as humans look to leaders for clear guidance during emergencies, dogs benefit from structured instruction that fosters security and cooperation.

Clear Expectations Reduce Stress

Dogs thrive in environments where rules and expectations are consistent. Leadership-based training creates a predictable framework that alleviates anxiety and builds confidence. By blending positive reinforcement with clear guidance, this method ensures dogs understand what is expected of them, reducing stress-related behaviours such as excessive barking or aggression. The result is a calm, balanced dog who feels secure within their environment.

Responsiveness Builds Trust

Leadership-based training is deeply attuned to a dog's emotional needs. By pairing responsive interaction with structured expectations, this method builds a sense of safety and partnership. Trust is established as dogs learn that their handlers provide not only rewards but also the guidance they need to feel secure. This trust encourages dogs to cooperate willingly and enthusiastically, rather than through fear or compulsion.

Encourages Cognitive Development

Structured guidance enhances a dog's ability to solve problems and make thoughtful decisions. By incorporating operant and counter-conditioning techniques within a leadership framework, this method fosters resilience and adaptability. Dogs trained with leadership-based methods learn to navigate challenges effectively, as demonstrated by the research of Brubaker and Udell, which highlights the benefits of authoritative interaction on cognitive growth.

Practical Implications of the Research

The collective findings from these studies provide a clear roadmap for dog trainers and owners seeking effective, humane, and evidence-based methods. Leadership-based training is:

- **Versatile:** Effective across a range of temperaments and behavioural

challenges.
- **Sustainable:** Promotes long-term improvements without reliance on treats or harsh corrections.
- **Holistic:** Addresses both the behavioural and emotional needs of dogs.

By focusing on clear communication, consistent rules, and responsive interaction, leadership-based training offers a scientifically validated path to fostering well-adjusted, cooperative, and happy dogs.

The evidence is unequivocal: leadership-based training is not only humane but also scientifically proven to be effective. It achieves a scientifically sound balance between structure and empathy, fostering trust, resilience, and significant improvements in behaviour. Supported by a growing consensus in the scientific community and backed by rigorous studies alongside real-world applications, this approach has become a cornerstone of modern, evidence-based dog training. For those aiming to build a strong and trusting bond with their canine companions, leadership-based training offers scientifically validated tools for achieving lasting success.